DREYER

By Mark Nash

1977

NEW YORK ZOETROPE

31 EAST 12th / NEW YORK 10003

Published by /British Film Institute/81 Dean Street, London W1V 6AA

Film Availability Services
General Editor: Paul Willemen

Acknowledgments

Cover still: *Day of Wrath* (courtesy of Cinegate)

I would like to thank all those who made the production of this publication possible: the staffs of the British Film Institute (particularly David Meeker and Jeremy Boulton) and the Danish Film Museum. A special vote of thanks goes to Paul Willemen for his untiring efforts to make the text as 'readable' as possible.

All quotations from *Cahiers du Cinéma*, except those from interviews, were translated by Tom Milne; the essay by Frieda Grafe was translated by Robin Mann.

All texts are reprinted by permission.

ISBN 0 85170 068 3

Contents

I. Introduction

One of the significant features of our film culture over the past five years has been a certain blockage around the notion of authorship. The productivity of the *auteur* theory has been limited, as whole areas of cinematic practices fell outside its scope. Critics often fell back on the instinctive designation of artistic individuality unsubstantiated by actual analysis. This blocking of *auteur* analysis was brought about largely by the failure of the works analysed to correspond to the theoretical models used, and coincided with a more general awareness of the theoretical and political problems inherent in the limitations of structuralism. The work initiated by the Edinburgh Film Festival, *e.g.* in their publications on Raoul Walsh and Jacques Tourneur[1] constituted an attempt to reformulate these problems in terms of textual practice with the emphasis shifting onto the relations, the *process* of signification, rather than the value or 'meaning' of particular discrete signifying units that can be isolated in the filmic discourse. This work essentially tried to dialecticise the ailing *auteurist*-structuralist model and open out the questions which it repressed or was otherwise unable to pose, questions which foreground the problems of reading and text construction.

Other recent developments in the Edinburgh Film Festival, which is one of the most progressive institutions in British film culture and an accurate index of advances in work on/in cinema, have evidenced a further series of shifts in the concepts deployed and the ways in which the object of study has been redefined. As the introduction to the *Edinburgh '76 Magazine*, no. 1, stated: '. . . the positivist separation between film as an object of study and the politics of film culture [became] progressively untenable . . . The key issue at stake was film as an ideological practice rather than as a predetermined and self-sufficient object of study. It was not until recently that the question of film as a signifying practice, of film as a process of articulation, tracing relations of subjectivity within film texts which themselves are embedded in the discourse of ideologies present in a given social formation, has been systematically examined).[2]

The Brecht event in '75, informed by the at that time widely available work of Althusser, indicated a rearticulation of notions of the politics of cinematic and critical discourses. The limitations of the unitary notion of ideology became apparent in attempts to extend Althusser's work on ideology[3] to the discourse of criticism. The event underlined the necessity to contest the undoubted hegemony in film culture of the journalistic discourse

1

of the majority of newspaper and magazine writers on film, and to fight control of that discourse over models of reading available to audiences. It has been clear for a long time that this discourse was deeply implicated in the diverse and often contradictory interests of the international film industry but it was impossible to work out the terms of that implication within a theoretical framework which did not allow sufficient autonomy to the ideological as a specific set of practices containing (in the active and passive senses of the verb) specific contradictions. Consequently, that theoretical framework, at best producing excellent formal analyses, was unable to tackle the fundamentally political nature of the hegemonic journalistic discourse on cinema, to analyse the specifics of the contradictions within it, its relation to the industry and to ideological hegemony in general. As a result, there were insuperable difficulties preventing the development of concrete strategies for ideological struggles in relation to the cinematic institution. Current, still ongoing work such as that of the Edinburgh Film Festival, *Screen* and the Independent Filmmakers' Association, arising from post-Althusserian reformulations of notions of ideology and the state, is beginning to enable work towards an altogether more political understanding of these problems.

While it is important that critical texts investigate the functioning of the cinematic institution and consolidate the transformation of theoretical space from the object cinema to the operation cinema, they can only have progressive effects if consciously articulated with their surrounding co-text, *e.g.* the contradictory shifts in production, distribution and exhibition within the industry marked by the work of the Independent Filmmakers' Association towards an oppositional/independent cinema, the emergence of the Association of Independent Producers and the opening of several independently owned cinemas, which, together with the Regional Film Theatres linked to the British Film Institute, offer the possibility of a viable 'third circuit' (with the precedents of the 'alternative' circuits of distribution of workers' films as well as Government sponsored films in the 30s and 40s). Unfortunately, at present this development is still wide open to the institutionalisation of a British art cinema, an animal so far rarely seen on these islands, except in its European varieties.

One of the interesting features of the Dreyer-text is that it has been taken up both by the ideologues of art cinema and those working towards an independent cinema. Even though such work is, in some respects at least, hostile to the establishment notions of art as essentially the repository for those religious values (the experience of transcendence, etc.) which no longer function effectively enough within organised religion, but which now operate more indirectly, resurfacing in the realm of 'Art'.

It is important that we address ourselves to these problems, not only because of this possibility of a surge of relatively independently financed art-cinema features of the type which characterised European production in the 50s and 60s, but also because of the need to shift the focus of the critical discourse away from Hollywood in order to examine the specific features of the institution cinema as it operates in Europe. Moreover, one discourse of which the persistent and chameleon-like functioning is often ignored is that of religion as a determinant in the social formation. It is overlooked, disavowed, as if somehow it shouldn't still be there. Yet we know that the institution of the church has survived politically for longer than any other state apparatus, and we also know that religious ideology is a constant point of appeal for some of the most reactionary elements in our culture, as indicated by *e.g.* the recent prosecution of *Gay News* for religious blasphemy.

These notes on certain features of the Dreyer-text are concerned with the ideological processes of text construction played out in the space between the 'author' of the filmic discourse and the reader/viewer, and the structure and functioning of the subject Dreyer produced in this reading. As Claire Johnston points out[4], the central question raised for film theory by psychoanalysis is what kind of reader the text constructs: how does today's patriarchal ideology position the subject? The emphasis of the following essay is on a reading in this sense, and as such is anti-*auteurist*, *i.e.* against attributing an imaginary unity to the 'author'. The notion of the 'Dreyer-text' refers then to a process theoretically constructed/reconstructed, in the first place (but not exclusively, as other discourses necessarily impinge upon the way such a process is constructed) from the sets of signifying relationships proposed by the films signed Carl Th.Dreyer. The 'film-text', is to be understood as a construction at the intermediate level of the individual film, the provisional unity of a segment of the discourse.

It should also be said in this introduction that metropolitan film culture should no longer be seen as the only significant domain of political and theoretical work. The work of consolidating the advances made, the struggle against the tyrany of journalistic models of reading, by means of texts and genuinely critical programming (*e.g.* as is attempted by some Regional Film Theatres) is equally important if we are not to fall into elitist theoretical vanguardism. The structure of this booklet tries to bear these problems in mind by providing several points of entry, so that readers unfamiliar with Dreyer's work or with some of the concepts deployed in the first essay can start from some point in the 'dossier' and work their way to the beginning. It is also hoped that readers, whether they attend a full National Film Theatre retrospective of Dreyer's films or more selective regional screenings, will be able to engage productively with the features of the Dreyer-text to which this booklet attempts to draw attention. It goes without saying that I hope the theoretical and ideological implications of the analyses presented here will be of interest and helpful to anyone interested in reading films and changing today's film culture, regardless of the degree of any individual's cathexis to Dreyer's films.

Notes

1. *Raoul Walsh*, ed. Phil Hardy, EFF 1974; *Jacques Tourneur*, ed. Claire Johnston and Paul Willemen, EFF 1975.
2. For further elaboration of this issue see the last few volumes of *Screen* and all Edinburgh Festival publications since 1974.
3. 'Ideology and Ideological State Apparatuses' in *Lenin and Philosophy*, London 1971.
4. *Edinburgh Magazine*, '76.

II. Notes on the Dreyer-text

A. 'In the beginning was the picture' (Dreyer).
'I am looked at, that is, I am a picture' (Lacan).

My interest in the cinema and in the functioning of cinematic texts is in understanding the ways in which cinema functions as an institution in conjunction with other institutions in the social formation. I study this institution not so much because I am fascinated by film, but because that fascination is an essential aspect of our production as ideological subjects.

There are no subjects outside of ideology and outside of the social formation, and while 'orthodox' Marxism has been relatively successful in its analyses of the political and economic areas of the social formation, the area of the ideological has proved much more problematic. It is in this area of our trying to come to terms with the functioning of the ideological, that psychoanalysis intervenes (though in a manner which is as yet conceptually difficult), attempting to provide some understanding of our production as speaking subjects: biological individuals with an identity constituted in language. The fictional nature of that identity was theorised by Freud with his discovery of the unconscious, and it was the work of Lacan which made possible the linking of that discovery with the work of linguistics, showing how the unconscious is produced in language. Ideology functions in such a way as to present us with a series of fictions: 'we' in our assumed identities 'are' those fictions, fictions which are constantly fissuring (the evidence of parapraxes, dreams neuroses etc). The work of ideology is to paper over these cracks, to shore up the fissuring edifice.

The discussion of the mechanisms of this operation of ideology have been in terms of the process of *suture*. This term has a history of use in anatomy. In the words of Stephen Heath: 'a stitching or tying as in the surgical joining of the lips of a wound', it also refers to the point at which articulations between bones (particularly those of the cranium) harden, are held together protecting the organism against fragmentation under physical stress. In addition, the word has a history of use in relation to literary composition, so its extension to the functioning of ideology within the cinematic text is not without precedent.

The functioning of ideology is then to be discussed in terms of this suturing function which has been developed by Lacan to mean a join between the orders of the Imaginary and the Symbolic, creating a fictional

5

identification, a pseudo-identification, for the subject. These terms need some further comment. The reader may be aware of the three areas of the Symbolic, the Imaginary and the Real which in Lacanian analytic theory co-exist and intersect in the subject. The Symbolic function is primary in the sense that it is the sphere of the production of the subject in language, (no Symbolic, no subject). Its functioning however is always modified by the Imaginary, it always acts in conjunction with the Imaginary. Without the simultaneous use of these two correlative functions the subject would have no experience of the Real. Symbolisation is not possible without Imaginary support and for our purposes these functions are perhaps best understood as two forces, the vectoral product of which 'is' the subject produced in a particular ideological 'direction'. (N.B. 'The psychoanalytic subject for Lacan . . . *is* not any *thing*, is defined topologically and not punctually, is the action of a structure' (Stephen Heath)[1]. Ideological representation then turns on, supports itself from the production of the subject in the Symbolic order, and directs this production as a set of images and fixed positions, fictions of coherence. Stephen Heath points out that suture functions in the cinematic text to 'bind the spectator as subject in the realisation of the film's space'. The spectator is bound to the image-frame and to the narrative in such a way that his/her fictional coherence as subject is maintained: 'The functioning of suture in image, frame, narrative, etc. is exactly a *process*: it counters a productivity, an excess that it states and restates in the very moment of containing in the interests of coherence' (Stephen Heath)[2].

One of the figures of that constraint to which I want to draw attention is Dreyer's celebrated attention to decor, the presentation within the diegesis, (the realm of the narrative's signified, the fictional world) of furniture, *objets d'art*, mirrors and paintings, and the way these participate in a 'freezing' of the flow of the film, a reinscription of stasis and centrality. In *Michael* this functions in terms of the reinscription of frame within the frame, in the use of paintings in the diegesis and the reduplication of the subject's relation to the visual field in the representation of a process of exchange between the characters in the diegesis and these frames within the frame: the paintings of Zoret, the comments of his friends, the reviews of the press.

The question of desire is also important in relation to the discussion of suture. As Claire Johnston points out: 'Desire is essentially the difference between satisfaction sought and satisfaction obtained. The object of desire is thus the memory trace of a previous gratification which can never be attained, but will always be the lost object forever reincarnating itself in a series of objects. Desire is set in motion with the first cry and the posing of the first signifier and with it a series of signifiers which are interchangeable, generating a perpetual metonymy, described by Laplanche and Leclaire as a scar, by its inexhaustible power of displacement made precisely to mark and mask the gap through which desire originates and into which it perpetually plunges'[1]. This metonymy is what is in play in the cinematic text tracing desire in image flow and narrative, the metonymic play of desire aiming to suture over the lack, the absence. In the film's movements, 'its framings, its cuts, its intermittences, the film ceaselessly poses an absence, a lack which is ceaselessly recaptured for—one needs to be able to say 'forin'—the film' (Stephen Heath)[1]. The process of desire set up, set going by this structuring of absences that is film, effects the suture while undermining it. It generates the excess which constantly threatens to overwhelm the subject and which in turn generates additional symbolic constraints, frames within the frame, a centering of the image. In this initial section of my essay I want to focus on three signs of desire in *Michael*, the paintings already referred to and the English glasses, both at the level of the narrative, and in addition the process of the look which they articulate and help inscribe in the diegesis.

An early scene in *Michael* concentrates on a picture, The Victor, painted by Zoret, a great artist modelled according to Dreyer on Rodin. It represents a young man, barely clothed, with arms outstretched towards the viewer in a possibly defiant pose. It is also indirectly a portrait of his model, Michael. This painting circulates through the diegesis, the framed gesture an image of excess constrained, contained. Zoret gives the painting to Michael who in turn sells it to help the Princess Zamikow who happens to be in financial difficulty. Zoret, hearing about this, insists on buying it back ('the price is immaterial') and having it rehung in Michael's room. Other paintings circulate in the diegesis: the Algerian sketches, the portrait of Zamikow, and the Job in the final tryptich which particularly functions to hold the spectator to the frame, centred in close shots in front of the audience come to view the masterwork. Paintings circulate as part of the narrative, containing, 'summing up' its flow. They also function simultaneously as signs of desire, representing a love object: Michael, Zamikow, or the process of desire itself (the 'Job'). Their cash value represents a particular modality of desire. Zoret, already a 'master', refuses the Princess's commission to paint her portrait. He doesn't need the money, because to him, money is a means of holding Michael, the object of his desire. In that sense, Zoret controls the money, he already has it. Michael's position is the inverse. He constantly seeks to distance himself from Zoret by appropriating his money, converting his paintings into money, a process Zoret finally stops in the finality of his death when all of his possessions pass to Michael (the text understands 'possess' in the sexual sense, an indirect representation of homoerotic relations: Zoret's love only achieves its aim in his death). That Zoret changes his mind and agrees to paint Zamikow is because she appears momentarily in Michael's position as object of desire, she suddenly 'looks' attractive, *i.e.* her eyes and body begin to reflect more light, paralleling Michael's appearance to Zoret several years before (Zoret had rejected him as an artist: 'Your sketches are no good, come back when you've learned to see', but then 'saw' his possibilities as a model). The portrait of Zamikow represents Zoret's attempt to suture, refurbish his desire for Michael. He attempts a relationship with her, in effectively excluding Michael from the dinner, but she is no more than Michael's stand-in.

This dinner is the occasion for the appearance of another sign of desire: the English glasses. They inaugurate a festival of luminous photography,

7

Zamikow and Zoret turning the glasses in their hands, savouring their properties in the light (cut-glass, along with painting and cinema depends for its 'life' on light), savouring the wine poured into them. Later in the narrative these same glasses are 'borrowed' by Michael also to entertain Zamikow, but placed in his room, with the row of childhood toys which is also Zoret's (*i.e.* supported by his money) and with The Victor hanging on the wall, they don't have quite the same effect. The glasses celebrate the succession of couples: Zoret/Zamikow, excluding Michael and Michael/Zamikow excluding Zoret. The third time they are mentioned, when Zoret wishes to celebrate a by now infrequent visit from Michael, the absence of the glasses indicates that this is not a return to the couple Zoret/Michael, but rather signifies the effective absence of Michael, the impossibility of Zoret to communicate with him. These glasses function as signifiers of desire, they are co-present with desire, predicated on the absence of the loved one, the separation of Michael and Zoret: they are absent from the diegesis when Zoret and Michael are together and they appear for the—illusory—formation of other couples.

Both the paintings and the glasses are stand-ins for and attempt to suture the forever renewed absence of the object of desire, of which Michael is the privileged sign. Michael passes from Zoret to Zamikow as a sign of their desire, and the narrative of the film is essentially the narrative of his passage from the field of Zoret's gaze to that of Zamikow's: her gaze ensnares him, as in the close shot of her eyes when she is sitting for her portrait. But that passage from an implicit homosexuality to the narcissistic/imaginary capture by the mother's face in his relation to Zamikow (who 'mothers' him and cradles him in her arms) is in fact no more than a passage from one modality of imaginary capture to another, represented in the mirroring correspondence in the names Z/oret-Z/amikow. The paintings can all be said to be about the absence of Michael, or rather about the presence of desire in the absence of its object. Zoret sets the narrative in motion with his project of painting 'Caesar as he was murdered by his adopted son Brutus', figuratively and symbolically anticipating his death by Michael's hand. This picture is mentioned in conversation but never seen, perhaps because the desiring relation is absent: it would represent Zoret already dead, when the process of the film is about his dying (for love); and the tableau of his death is a representation of Zoret killed by Michael's effect on him, *i.e.* killed by desire.

What is common to the paintings, the glasses and Michael as signs of desire is their function within a system of exchange based on the look and the light which supports it. This process is foregrounded in an early scene in the film when Zoret shows Zamikow his paintings. In that scene, Michael is told by Zoret to carry a spotlight and to shine it on The Victor, the painting for which he modelled. Turning to Michael, Zamikow recognises 'the original'. Zoret draws her attention onward, to another frame, another scene, this time a romantic heterosexual embrace, suggesting a transposition of Rodin's sculpture *The Kiss* into a pictorial form. While the two of them engage the painting in their gazes, Michael runs the light from the painting over Zamikow's body, returning the movement of her sexually appraising gaze.

Light itself can function as signifier which, through a metaphoric process, stands for desire. The text privileges it in this way in a number of instances: Michael's entry, at a dramatic moment in the ballet Swan Lake, haloed in a beam of light which penetrates the depth of the auditorium up to the stage, exactly like the projector's beam in a film theatre; the scene where he relaxes by an open window, bathed in light (originating metonymically in his embrace with Zamikow in the previous scene), with Switt to his right and Zoret facing the two of them (*i.e.* Zoret's past and present lovers illuminated) with a fountain suggestively playing in the foreground. Michael's departure is equated in the text with the blocking of light, the closing of the shutters, the blocking of communication with Zoret, as when the chess board is sent away. Another instance of the privileging of light occurs in relation to the Algerian sketches, which to Zoret represent the finest memories of his time with Michael. They are dominated by the effects of light to the exclusion of figures, and it is this same light effect which Zoret used in his final painting representing the biblical figure Job, symbolising the effects of his desire for Michael.

The many scenes of viewing in the film function as analogous to the acts of viewing of the film by another set of spectators whose eyes are directed by beams of light at images, *i.e.* the audience. Similarly, the scene of the painting of Zamikow's portrait rehearses this process of image construction with the painter/director organising a field of visual marks in a frame. In this instance, it is a double movement of inscription into the visual discourse of that which disturbs the desiring relation between Zoret/Michael: the female body. The object fixed in the visual field of the eye of the painter is also that which is privileged by the eye of the camera, and by extension, of the director as the organiser of the filmic discourse. The diegetic figure of Zamikow, object of desire fixed and contained in the painting, is also the sequined body of Nora Gregor, already radiant with anticipated stardom. The star-system, founded on the structure of fetishism, producing a fetish for the film and for the viewer, doubly contained in the film-frame and the painting within it, thus doubly inscribed as 'disturbance to be contained', doubly threatening, doubly fetishistic. Further—the use of the spotlight to throw light on the painting parallels the process of filming (lighting a set) and the process of film viewing, the projector beam redoubled by the viewer's gaze. In other words, the structuring of the diegetic story enlightens us about the cinematic process, reflecting the process of construction of a visual discourse back at us.

'The look is outside because "I am looked at, that is, I am a picture" the subject sees and is seen and is instituted in that dialectic, the dialectic of eye and look which can know no coincidence' (Stephen Heath)[3]. Zoret, Zamikow and Michael are all looked at by intradiegetic spectators and the extradiegetic viewer, and they become, literally, pictures. Michael was one already at the beginning of the diegesis in the painting entitled The Victor.

In their attempts to materialise the act of seeing, paintings 'materialise' the object in the field of the look, attempting to grasp the 'reality' in front of the eye in a representation. The look as object of desire constantly eludes attempts to capture it. It cannot be represented, except marginally, *e.g.* the marginality of the side panels of the tryptich, the looks of/at the side panels elided in the framing of the central panel as if it were a single painting. Another example can be found in *Vampyr*: David Grey's look at himself looking, marginalised into a structure of uncertainty[4]. This marginality is equally evident in the oblique return of the viewers'/painter's gaze by figures in the paintings, paralleling the discretion of matching gazes in classic shot-reverse-shot configurations. It is the marginality, says Lacan, of the infant's turning towards a person present but not directly implicated in its game of looks with its mirror image. The attempt of painting to trap the look, freeze excess and fix desire only results in their becoming objectified, alienated and therefore available for entry into the circuit of financial exchange, only to be replaced by a new painting. The act of painting only finishes with the final tableau: Zoret's death.

B. 'The dramatisation of the structure of phantasy plus the introduction of the founding lack which marks the entry into the symbolic produces a text which appears to be the dramatisation of desire itself, the tracing of desire over/in the body of the text' (Paul Willemen).

The look, as the object of phantasy in the scopic field institutes the subject in the visible, or rather the subject is instituted in the visible on the trace (with its double sense of 'mark' and 'search') of the look. It cannot be seized because the subject's existence is predicated on it. The 'evanescent' property of the look is foregrounded in *Michael* with its play on light as material signifier of the look, penetrating darkness, surrounded by absence. In this respect, the look as that which bridges and thus also signifies the divide between two terms (the looker and that which is looked at), functions as a signifier of desire. Some representation of absence always circulates in the Dreyer-text—within the frame there is always some kind of barrier, something which bars access to the fictional world whether it is a reduplication of framing as in *Michael*, a dark halo surrounding the lit scene, or the 'barred' image as in *Day of Wrath* (see cover), or some articulation of the two as in *Gertrud*. Further study of the text will elucidate other articulations, but the basic structure of the institution of a lack, of some signifier of separation, persists.

That ceaseless displacement of signifiers of desire—Zoret cannot render Zamikow's eyes, he cannot 'get' them, the English glasses are elsewhere when he wants them—also applies to the presence of Michael, all evanescent carriers of Zoret's desire which is ceaselessly renewed by the absence they represent. Zoret's desire appears to be predicated on Michael's absence.

10

Michael does not desert him, rather in order for Zoret to love he must first be deserted, so that when he repeats as he is dying, the motto of the film: 'Now I can die in peace, having known a great love', he also states the central process structuring the diegesis. The interest of the film resides precisely in its ability to represent so 'clearly' this constant slipping of the object of desire, this constant attempt to possess through looks, to find a desirable 'I' in the eyes/objects which, by being subjected to a look, locate the 'looker'.

The process of the subject, its production and placing in and by the text, hinges in *Michael* on Zoret as the authorial representative. It is in relation to him that the problematic of looking and of its concomitant, the construction of images, functions. But this process is also one of subjection (the paintings produce the artist in the same way that images produce the viewer) and of suffering, in that the process only continues to function on the basis of the repetition of absence and separation, *i.e.* the repetition of loss. In religious terms, it is total loss—Job/Zoret, 'A man who has lost everything . . . Vivat Claude Zoret'—which for Job also constitutes the state of Grace, that tamed and oppressive version of ultimate joy (*jouissance*). In the scene where the 'painter of suffering' is offered 'the glory of our country' in the form of the *Légion d'honneur* or some such decoration conventionally the object of male bourgeois ambition, the medal firstly serves as a marker of Michael's absence: the medal is 'meaningless' because Michael is not there to witness the ceremony. The image produces the artist, but this process of 'subject production' needs the sanction of a third: the look of the witness. The medal bestowed upon Zoret acts only as the signifier of the absence of that look. The child seeing its I in the mirror, looks at the mother to guarantee the relation of subjectivity thus instituted; but Zoret, although he had his mirror (the Job—painting) misses the look in return from his object of desire, Michael. This absence is also what causes Zoret's mirror, his painting, to reflect the desolate figure of Job, the christian symbol of utter loss, back at him.

The sexual ambiguity present throughout the film in the homoerotic values inherent in the relationship is crystallised in this scene, but the terms are reversed. Zoret-the-master becomes Zoret-the-infant anxiously seeking the look of Michael, who thus comes to occupy the place usually occupied by the mother. This reversal also highlights indirectly the problematic which the film text poses and, unsuccessfully, attempts to contain: that of bisexuality. Although bisexuality was primarily carried by the figure of Michael (in relation to the Zoret/Zamikow nexus), the oscillation of Zoret between father and infant adumbrates the same problematic. In a third movement (the play of looks and the implied play of sexed identifications being the first two), the founding problematic of bisexuality is re-inscribed into the film-text quite explicitly, though marginalised. The tryptich of which Job occupies the central panel is at times, almost accidentally, seen *in toto*, even though shots of the tryptich invariably present the figure of Job as the whole painting. In fact, the Job panel is framed by paintings of a young male and a young woman, as if he were caught in the divide between male/female, a divide crossed by their looks, a space in between sexed identities where the sexual indeterminacy of old age echoes that of infancy. But it is in fact a sexual indeterminacy partaking of both sexes: the Job painting is still part and parcel of the tryptich, it is not an isolated, autonomous work. Moreover, the reversal in relation to age mentioned above (*i.e.* Zoret and Michael) is also echoed in the painting: it is traditionally the child which is caught and placed in the intersection of the male and female parental looks; instead, in the painting, the place of the parents is occupied by images of youth, while the place of the infant is occupied by old Job. But the film text necessarily marginalises this barely masked representation of the problematic of bisexuality: the price the representation pays for its presence in the text is precisely its marginality, its incidental, accidental emergence in long shots ostensibly motivated by the psychological logic of the story which 'requires', at that point, that Zoret be shown isolated in a crowd.

'In every man who speaks of the absence of the other ['Where is Michael?'], the feminine declares itself: he who waits and suffers is miraculously feminised. A man is not feminised because he is homosexual, but because he is in love' (Barthes)[5]. *Michael* foregrounds the (necessarily repressed) bisexual drive of the spectator in relation to the scopic drive, polarising it in terms of the conventional hetero/homosexual dichotomy. This process can be traced in Michael's fascination with and his distanciation from his own image and in his confusion between ideal ego (image of himself) and ego ideal (Zoret). It also functions in Zoret's scopic contact with the objects of his desire: Michael and Zamikow' (an unsuccessful transition from Michael), inscribed on behalf of the author in the privileged lighting of both their bodies. What surfaces in the viewer and is reinscribed into the figure of Zoret, is that feminisation attendant on waiting, the waiting attendant on absence, the flow of desire. The feminisation could be read in terms of the traces in the diegesis of the expulsion of overt homosexuality. The text's avoidance of any direct representation of homosexuality is not just because it is also avoided in Herman Bang's novel, nor because of the socio-moral codes which surrounded both novelistic and filmic productions, but rather because there is a discretion necessary to the text for it to put absence in play, a vacillation of subject position between the terms of 'author' and 'viewer'[6]. The vacillation, the uncertainty of position producing on the level of sexed identity a similar uncertainty and vacillation. In this sense, what is repressed, and therefore represented in the interstices of the text, is not homosexuality, the faithful shadow of heterosexuality. It is bisexuality which constitutes the trouble of the text and generates and organises its complete set of displacements and exchanges.

C. The barred image

In *Day of Wrath*, Anne's face is invariably shown in partial shadow up to the point where she asserts her own desire, when her face becomes literally radiant, reflecting light. This turning point, this access to sexuality is marked by her change in dress, the laughing and singing, and her needlework design showing a woman leading a child by the hand and an apple tree with a single blossom. The connection of sexual repression with this 'barred' lighting effect is made particularly clear in the shot of her watching Marthe Herlof being burnt (see cover). The window forms a bar over her face, the light from the fire (where a desiring woman is being consumed—the same light which will soon be seen in Anne's eyes) casting shadows on it. This barring, the signifier of repression, reappears in a different register in *Ordet*, *e.g.* in the check pattern of the dress Inger wears about the house. It is also the pattern of the table cloth on which she cuts special biscuits and on which she is later lain and herself cut in the difficult delivery of her stillborn child. A potentially productive female body precisely 'in check'.

At the end of the first reel of *Day of Wrath* when Anne enters the church, a long tracking shot follows her as she spies on her husband Absalom's interrogation of Marthe, who has been accused of witchcraft. A balancing camera movement follows Anne's return through the aisles while choirboys are heard singing the *Dies Irae*. Martin, her stepson, enters and explains to her that the music is for the burning of Marthe. We see the score of the music in close-up obscured by the shadow of the choir master: the shadow, the bar of symbolic restraint. Anne says she can already hear Marthe's shrieks, which then appear on the sound track as we cut to a slow pan round the torture chamber. This can be taken as a nodal point in the film from which a structural feature of the Dreyer-text can be deciphered. It is the only point at which what I call the 'barred image' denotes potential threat (of torture), as in the convention of the horror film where 'such black areas usually signify that some dangerous object or person could emerge from those blind spots at any time' (Paul Willemen)[7]. If this torture sequence is examined in detail and compared for instance with Jacques Tourneur's *mise-en-scène*, some significant differences come to light. The areas of darkness hide much less than either the camera's edging away from the scene of torture, the implication of the screams-off, etc. Shadows in Dreyer rarely go beyond grey, they do not really hide anything, but on the contrary indicate that there is nothing to hide (the kind of reassurance a night-light provides in a child's bedroom), or rather they indicate that there is a problem around the presence/absence of light such that the full field of its presence is marked by certain traces of its absence, shadows.

This leads to a suggestion of a central organising phantasy in the Dreyer-text, in which light becomes a representation within the space of the frame of the act of looking itself, the active incidence of light on the space demarcated by the edges of the frame. In this context, this space can be seen as the space

13

of phantasy, the imaginary space in which the play of subject production is enacted via a set of shifting identifications and projections. In other words, the space of the frame which always necessarily includes a relation with the one for whom it constitutes a space (*i.e.* the viewer), becomes analogous to the body of the mother, the Imaginary other who functions as the privileged object of desire, the locus from which total satisfaction can/will emanate and whose presence/absence constitutes the limit of the subject: the subject needs the presence of this other so that separation from it may acquire the significance necessary for the subject to come into being. In this way, the incidence of light onto the (maternal) body represented by the screen image (a succession of frames from which even the dividing gaps have been erased to produce/preserve an imaginary plenitude) stands as the material trace, the signifier of the relation between looker/look/object. In other terms, the specific inscription of light in the Dreyer-text functions as the signifier of desire (the look), binding the viewer into the framework of a phantasy structure.

A similar process was analysed in relation to Raoul Walsh's *Pursued*,[8] where the Western phantasy was found to be organised around the verb 'to shoot'. In Dreyer, the phantasy appears to operate around 'light' as a material visual signifier of the look, generating, metaphorically, plots about divine light and semantic structures organising a variety of permutations on the concept (*i.e.* signified) of 'light': the fire of passion versus divine light, the ordered light of reason versus the flickering flames of desire, light versus dark versions of christianity as well as the various types of absence of light (see my earlier remarks about the function of shadows in Dreyer's films). Yet in the insistence on the light of vision, that nothing escape the eye (shadows which mark but do not hide), on the absence of lack, have we not reached the phantasy of the phallic mother generated at the moment when the child becomes uncertain whether the mother does (still) possess/is the phallus? This castration-anxiety appears to be displaced into the act of looking itself and the blotting or barring of the visual field operates as a mark, a trace of the subject's separation from the imaginary plenitude which existed 'before' and which persists as an ongoing temptation. These incestuous fantasies, which (male) creativity relieves and relives, are structured by the doubly signifying presence of light representing both the child and the parent's act of looking: in the phantasy of the primal scene the child looks on and is caught in the act of looking by a returned look, re-enforcing the symbolic and painful separation from the object of his/her desire. The play of identifications open to the child in that phantasy situation being an important element in the construction of the sexed identity of the child: identification with the mother producing female positions, with the father male positions, regardless of the biological sex of the infant. Both types of indentification representing strategies to escape the painful experience of exclusion, of separation. In the Dreyer-text, the identifications proposed produce male positions in that the light, the signifier of the look, functions in relation to objects of desire troubled by their positioning as females. Or

14

rather, troubled by the socio-cultural presuppositions and constraints attendant upon being placed as female in a strongly patriarchal order.

The 'communicational model' developed in relation to the institution of cinema in Paul Willemen's above mentioned analysis of *Pursued*, can, in a general sense, be applied to the Dreyer-text which foregrounds authorial marks, *e.g.* the system of pronoun functions and interventions I analysed in *Vampyr*[9]. In the *Pursued* analysis, it is the process of the text which constructs within a historically determined context, the 'reader' and the 'author' as agencies where each constructs their fantasy of the other. 'This conception of the subject (the one time author)' writes Willemen, 'may appear bewildering, but in fact any interview of a director or a viewer will show evidence of this: the director's referring to what viewers 'want', viewers referring to the 'world' of the author and holding him/her accountable for notions the reader him/herself produced in the very act of reading'. Such a model is clearest in *Michael* with its diegetic foregrounding of the discourse of art and its implicit parallels with film-making. Although this has wideranging consequences for the analysis of other films by Dreyer, it is perhaps necessary to elaborate a little on the general model. In the analysis of *Pursued*, we read: 'As soon as the 'signified subject' makes its appearance, it immediately freezes into a mark of itself, *i.e.* into another signifier, the subject fading away once more, eternally ungraspable except in its elusive and deceptive effects'. Now this 'constant freezing' which applies to the process of painting in *Michael* also applies to the field of the frame where such freezing can be traced in the emphasis on composition, aesthetics and the order of the signifier in general. In fact critics constantly return to this effect in the form of comparisons between the organisation of the visual field of Dreyer's films and painting. For instance, Bazin compared *Day of Wrath's* compositions to Dutch 17th century painting and a Danish reviewer compared *Ordet* to the 'quiet' interiors of the 19th century Danish painter Hammershøj. This process also operates at the syntagmatic level— the succession of 'frozen' tableaus, the restrained rhythm, the carefully orchestrated dislocation of character point-of-view with that of the authorial 'I', etc.

We can also speculate (speculation: the creative assumption by the viewer of the dialectical relation between 'author' and 'reader' the text sets up) on the parallelism of cinema, particularly so-called art cinema, and the institution of religious discourse. The cinema puts in play the viewer's phantasy of the director, the author of the discourse, in an attitude paralleling the 16th century doctrine of signatures: 'It is not God's will that what he creates for man's benefit and what he has given us should remain hidden . . . And even though he has hidden certain things, he has allowed nothing to remain without exterior and visible signs in the form of special marks—just as a man who has buried a hoard of treasure marks the spot where he may find it again' (Paracelsus: *The Nature of Things*); 'Just as the secret movements of His understanding are manifested by His voice, so it would seem that the herbs speak to the curious physician through their signatures, discovering to him . . . their inner virtues hidden beneath nature's veil of silence' (Crollius: *Treatise on Signatures*)[10]. The viewer, 16th century physician/20th century spectator, reads the marks that 'God' has inscribed, and re-constructs Him from his traces.

This process, following the strategy of the Dreyer-text in foregrounding the signifying processes of the text in its construction of 'reader' and 'author', is often diegetically represented in Dreyer's films in terms of a religious discourse[11]. In *Ordet*, the articulation of light and dark within the frame is presented diegetically in terms of 'light' and 'dark' (Dreyer's phrases) versions of Christianity, Grundtvigian versus the Inner Mission. The Inner Mission is presented negatively, its 'dark' destructive potential originating in its adherents who are persuaded to declare the inner conviction that they are destined for salvation, indeed that they are already saved (note the testimony of Mette Martin, who has found this God in her rejection of sin— read sexuality—and who speaks with the same hypnotic delivery as Gertrud, another woman whose words are not her own), whereas the life at Borgensgaard is axed around the issue of belief: does God exist or not? (Mikkel, the doctor); what can be read as a trace of His presence? (Inger and her daughter Karen, who believe in 'daily' miracles); Old Borgen and the pastor who doubt or disbelieve. The intolerability of Johannes' assertion that he is the risen Christ is due to his removing the space for doubt, the possibility of distance from God, the uncertainty about His interventions, even His existence, all of them paradoxically the implicit conditions for believing in Him and loving Him. Religion underscores Barthes' assertion of the lover's need for the uncertainty of absence[12].

The main interest of the Dreyer-text is that, although caught up in the traditional theological view of cinema with its 'god-like' author, mysteriously present 'everywhere', *i.e.* nowhere, it nevertheless presents this ideology as a highly problematic one. Dreyer played the game: the 'tyrannical Dane' who ordains (orders, decrees) the processes constructing the films, a God rejecting any creation others interfered with (*e.g. Two People*) yet manifesting his own uncertainty about his paternal status.

It is the uncertainty, the oscillations, in short, the 'trouble' haunting the Dreyer-text which makes it such a productive signifying process and as this trouble is none other than the impossibility to totally repress/resolve the problem of bisexuality within a rigidly patriarchal culture, the structures set up to try and deal with it produce texts that directly engage with the fundamental issues at stake in the cinematic institution: the relationship between the sets of signifiers which constitute cinematic discourse, involving all its materials of expression (sound, writing, music, images, speech) and the division within each set between on the one hand its Order, its systematicity and on the other its repressed, its excess.

D. I. One of the problems that has beset Marxist attempts to relate artistic production to general economic production has been the base-superstructure model in which works of art and in some versions language, are mere reflections of a socio-economic base. This theoretical reduction of ideology to an unproblematic reflection has facilitated the persistence of romantic ideologies of the individual artist supposedly outside of or marginal to society. Another result was that it opposed or misrepresented the kind of work with which *e.g.* the name of Brecht is usually associated, because it challenges idealist practices with work which can participate in the struggle to change consciousness, recognising that artistic practices have their own levels of specificity and are not simply a transcription of politics in another field. The work of Julia Kristeva[13] directly addresses this problem by posing the 'speaking subject' as the area where signifying practices and mode of production intersect, and by theorising the function of art as potentially subversive of the dominant conceptions of the speaking subject.

Kristeva develops the concept of signifying practice as a double movement, both a setting in place and a traversing or cutting through of a system of signs. This setting in place requires the identity of a speaking subject in a social institution recognised by this subject as the support of its identity. The opposite, traversing movement occurs when this speaking subject is put 'in process' and cuts across the social institutions in which it had previously recognised itself. In any mode of production, a signifying practice is that through which the mode of production signifies its stabilisation and its (self) expenditure, the condition of its renewal. In other less abstractly schematic terms, Kristeva's thesis is that the mode of production of a socio-economic ensemble and the mode of signification are intrinsically related, and that the speaking subject is the terrain on which this relationship acts itself out. A particular historical conjuncture will manifest a certain type of relation between unity and process, between the unity, the stasis of a system, and the process 'traversing' that system, cutting across its boundaries. In the second half of the 19th century, following the bourgeois revolutions, a particular unity of the state and family was achieved at the price of a specific, largely secularised strategy of repression/containment of desire; a strategy which consisted firstly in attempts to fix the fundamentally unstable, processual energy (flux) of desire and to contain it within the terms of coherent, totalising systems. In this way a dialectical process was set in motion perpetually re-ordering, re-organising systems in order to try and account for the libidinal energy which previous/other systems needed to expel or disavow. In his lucid introduction to Kristeva's essay, Geoffrey Nowell-Smith summarised some of the fundamental arguments underlying Kristeva's thesis. I will quote from this introduction at some length because a) the points I intend to make in relation to the Dreyer-text rely heavily on Kristeva's argument, and b) it is difficult to see how Nowell-Smith's formulations could be improved upon. He writes: 'Language, she argues, and with language a variety of signifying practices connected with either art or religion, is essential to human sociality, since the institution of social relations (production, reproduction) brings with it the co-institution of ways in which these (and other) relations are to be represented. The social animal is also a symbolic animal. Traditionally, however, symbolic relations have always been seen as somehow non-contradictory. They bind together the social organism, either masking its contradictions or, at most, reflecting them. For Kristeva, on the other hand, there is a basic contradictoriness immanent in symbolic relations themselves, parallel to, and closely connected with, the contradictions discerned by Marx at the level of the process of social production. Symbolic relations do not simply reflect 'real' relations. They are a necessary condition of existence of any sociality, but they are established only at the cost of a sacrifice, and the effects of this sacrifice continue to make themselves felt in the social body and to compound the antagonisms generated at the base. The crisis of social relations brought about by capitalism helps to determine a crisis already endemic in the symbolic forms through which these institutions are thought, and this second crisis, in the course of laying bare its own contradictions, also illuminates the contradictions of the social forms and the possibility of a revolution at both levels at once. It is here that Freud is brought to the aid of Marx. Crucial to Kristeva's argument is the notion of the human subject as site of symbolic practice, and as being set in place by the institutions through which it recognises its own identity. It is not a question of there being an 'individual' who comes to terms with 'society' and the 'real world'. Rather the subject is constructed through practices by which it finds itself from a position of alterity. This model of the constitution of the subject is a Freudian one, and Freudian too is the explanation Kristeva gives of the necessary sacrifice—'castration'—on which sociality is founded. In Kristeva's account the formation of a subject which finds its identity in social and symbolic institutions necessitates a division between a 'symbolic' area proper and another area to which she gives the name 'semiotic'. This semiotic area, analogous to the Freudian unconscious, is the site of those signifying or pre-signifying practices which do not take the form of signification in the linguistic sense and which language so to speak represses so that they can only emerge into the symbolic area in the form of interruptions of ordered discourse. Whereas the symbolic is a structure, the semiotic is a process, and in this process there is the constant production of an overflow whose release is experienced as pleasure (jouissance) in the course of the cutting across of the boundaries separating process and structure.

The division between the symbolic and the semiotic implies a critique of structural linguistics and of its central concept, the sign as union of signifier and signified. Whereas in structural linguistics (and structuralism generally) systems of signs are seen as autonomous wholes and as linking together the socio-economic and the physical instances, for Kristeva there is always something radically heterogeneous in the process she calls 'signifiance' (semiotic + symbolic). Signification (the binding of signifier and signified) she sees as only part of the overall process.

Although sign and signification exist (on the side of the symbolic) they are not pre-given concepts but effects of the division between semiotic and symbolic through which social identity is instituted. The constant re-working of the boundaries of social, psychical and signifying makes impossible any totalising project for a semiotics (in the linguists's sense) which would give a once and for all account of what signifying practices are and what they signify. Certain 'structuralist' pretensions therefore fall by the wayside, since their positivist bias fails to take account of the contradictions inherent in the process on which they themselves are founded.

The western episteme, it should also be noted, is patriarchal. Whether in Judaism or in Christianity, or for that matter in secular rationalism, the division between the homogeneous-symbolic and the semiotic which is heterogeneous to it, always sets the feminine on the side of the heterogeneity. The coincidence of language and patriarchy as foundations of sociality and identity makes woman literally the unnameable and the unsaid. As such the feminine—in so far as it can be spoken—has a profoundly subversive function. The danger of course is that the power of the division is such that it can only be breached at the risk of psychotic breakdown. Hence Kristeva's interest both in those avant-garde literary practices in the Capitalist West whose operations on language have got dangerously close to breaking down the barrier, and in the signifying practices in other modes of production where patriarchy is not instituted in the same way'.

It must be pointed out that Kristeva's concept of the symbolic is not the same as Lacan's. Indeed the order of the symbolic as presented by Kristeva would in Lacanian terms be closer to an Imaginary order (an attempt to unify, to render sets of relationships homogeneous), whereas Kristeva's semiotic manifests itself precisely in the site of Lacan's Symbolic: the drives break through in the fissures, the gaps, the absences, the exclusions upon which any Order is founded. In this sense the marks of the semiotic process in the order of language speak its absences, and are therefore allied to Lacan's Symbolic (the institution of separation, the assumption of castration upon which the subject is predicated).

To return to Dreyer, I will endeavour to show that the Dreyer-text can be read as an exemplary site where the discourses of religion, art and the feminine intersect. At the level of content, Dreyer's films rehearse the playing out of politico-religious doctrinal struggles within the context of a patriarchal order marked by Judaeo-Christian monotheism: the problems of anti-semitism in *Love One Another* and the projected Jesus-film; witchcraft in *Day of Wrath, Joan of Arc, The Parson's Widow, Vampyr*; catholicism and the crucifixion in *Leaves from Satan's Book*, the Jesus-film and the Mary Stuart project. It is most notably in *Ordet*, literally meaning *The Word*, and in *Gertrud* that the religious discourse is spun out across cinematic constructions which in return show up the closely complicit relation between the religious discourses and the languages of sexuality and art. The central question of the film, 'Who has it?' (*i.e.* the word), echoes the child's anxious questioning as to who has/is the phallus, with the oedipal drama as the scene in which the confusion between having/being is

19

supposed to be resolved in terms of questions relating to 'having'. The film's answer is equivocal: *not* the mother (Inger is not allowed her baby[14]), and yet a child, the mother's phallus separated from her, can be a vehicle for the Word.

In *Moses and Monotheism*, according to Kristeva[15], Freud suggests that Christianity, albeit through a misrecognition characteristic of religious discourse, comes near to a recognition of the act of murder involved in the founding of sociality. Rather than the son's murder of the father in Judaism, Christianity formulates this act of murder in terms of the murder of the son (the Crucifixion), where the word having become flesh returns to the father, ('thus speaks my church on earth . . . the church that has betrayed me, murdered me in my own name', *Ordet*). The force of Bataille's remark quoted by Kristeva: 'The truth of language is Christian', comes from this double movement in Christianity: the death and resurrection of the Word which comes close to a recognition of the process of loss in language, its structuring of absence. 'And the word became flesh': both the formula for conversion hysteria and the pointer to that linguistics of the Word which has had certain effects on semiotics and psychoanalysis, *e.g.* the emergence of a right-wing Lacanianism in France. A linguistics which cannot present an adequate theory of the drives, of the articulation of the Semiotic with the Symbolic. This fixation on the level of the word is put into play in the Dreyer-text. The French critic and now also filmmaker, A. Téchiné, perceptively remarked in relation to *Gertrud*: 'We know from Blanchot that speech replaces the concrete by an essential equilibrium close to immobility', action.* The film makes visible the final stages of the acquisition of the order of language, acknowledging the living movement from which it has become detached and with which it will never again merge.' Yet the film also makes immobility, sitting or standing, leaning against furniture etc. Yet within that same film, this weight of language is partially suspended by the infiltration of the drives into language in the form of the rhythm of the speech, intonation and music. As Téchiné writes: 'Words echo, tending to rhythm, away from action. The film makes visible the final stages of the acquisition of the order of language, acknowledging the living movement from which it has become detached and with which it will never again merge'. Yet the film also makes visible that this acquisition occurs at the price of a sacrifice: the men in the diegesis can speak but cannot love; women cannot identify with the order of language in that fashion. Gertrud's mother-in-law cannot remember what she has just been reading nor why she visits Gertrud and Kanning. The whole problematic of Gertrud's life is in her having been a singer destined to sing men's words, a contradiction she can't sustain. The emergence of the drives through the body of the Dreyer-text (diegetically through the body of Gertrud, for instance) demonstrates the relativisation of religious discourse faced with an other, another mode of introducing heterogeneity into the social ensemble, *i.e.* 'art'. As mentioned earlier, the process of the Dreyer-

*For the complete text of Téchiné's essay, see p 72 [Ed. note].

20

text derives its interest precisely from the clarity with which this articulation is presented. It suspends not only disbelief, the romantic precondition for the aesthetic, but also, in its religious signification, belief. The discourse of religion is relativised to the point where it invalidates any specifically religious readings of the films. Of course the catholic *Revue du Cinéma* was very interested in the use of Dreyer's films 'for the cause', but at the same time manifested some unease about possible contamination from his imagined Protestantism (as opposed to the protestantism with a small 'p' which his films do present).

In the 19th century crisis of finitudes that Kristeva discusses, art both takes over the function of religion as container of heterogeneity and, in the form of the avant-garde text contests the unity of the social ensemble that other artistic practices are complicit in attempting to re-establish. Art makes a 'game out of everything which has been a part of the repressed sector of society', but in doing so causes those repressed elements to speak out. Such a repressed sector which begins to speak out in the late 19th century is that of the feminine. We can note for instance in the Scandinavian literary culture from which Dreyer draws much of his material , preoccupations with women's social position and desire (Ibsen, Söderberg) and the implicit problem of homosexuality (Bang) initially raised at this time in terms such as 'the intermediate sex'[16] (*e.g.* 'the feminine mind in man') discussions of which are also linked to the repressive function of the 'Holy' family.

The return of the repressed feminine in signifying practices causes a crisis most easily read in verbal avant-garde practices where the subject produced by poetic language is produced under torsion, in male as well as female roles[15]. This process of subject production in poetic language does institute sexed roles, but it does so in a double edged manner: the production of meaning-for-a-subject in avant-garde practices inaugurates structure and identity, mastery and finitude, but it simultaneously undercuts this by means of processes multiplying and dispersing that meaning, opening it up to the force of semiotic, centrifugal drives culturally located on the side of the feminine, the maternal. A good example of this process is the role of rhythm in language and its relation of force to the order of syntax and meaning: it can be present as an undercurrent still dominated by the orderly signifying structure of grammatical language, or it can totally disrupt that order, exceeding the bounds of meaning and syntax, fragmenting the 'ordered' discourse even to the point where linguistic units are dispersed into a–signifying babble. In this sense, the texts still produce subjects as sexed, but ambiguously so. Poetic processes do not merge these subject positions but play on their very differentiation, oscillating between them, introducing heterogeneity into what would otherwise be regarded as homogeneously unified sex-identities. For Kristeva the modern avant-garde text points out that the family and the relations of re-production while functioning to maintain the stability of a particular social order, *also* demarcate the area within which the pleasure process is allowed to operate. Modern avant-garde texts interrogate the functions of paternity and sexual prohibitions associated with this familial nexus and foreground the (maternal) woman as the repressed bearer of pleasureable overflow. However, the incestuous pleasures thus evoked cannot be articulated directly without an accompanying shift in authorial position, either re-fetishising the mother to again make her inaccessible or identifying the place of the mother with the repressed, the unnameable.

Dreyer's films participate indirectly in this problematic of the modern text. The puritanism, the level of repression in the text of 'his' films is so extreme that sexuality can only be expressed indirectly through libidinal displacement, to produce a text which can be called a hysterical text, in many ways the counterpart to the (Victorian) hysterical body. The movement of this essay, tracing the symptoms of this displacement through the body of the Dreyer-text parallels the development of psychoanalysis which was founded on listening to the discourse of hysterics. And since I am talking about subject positions rather than individual subjects, these texts can be retrospectively included within the globality of hysterical discourse in relation to which psychoanalysis was and continues to be developed. My reading will atempt to show a similar shift under the pressure of the incest taboo towards an identification with the place of the mother as 'repressed/unnameable'.

The primary process is experienced by the child within the familial nexus in terms of melodic, rhythmic and intonational structures. His/her dependence on the mother is a semiotic one, which will later surface 'through' the use of language structure in the symbolic. According to Kristeva[17], the Chinese language illustrates in an exemplary manner this interaction of the semiotic and the symbolic: on the one hand there is the knowledge of grammar, logic and syntax belonging to the secondary process and the symbolic, but on the other there is a complex utilisation of the body, of kinaesthetic senses, important manifestations of the semiotic. Kristeva argues that this childhood relation to the mother is relived during the creative process in adulthood. The production of art reactivates the emotional trauma of transition away from the incestuous child-mother relationship in which the semiotic is dominant. In this respect, women experience the incestuous relationship in a specific manner, in that a level of identification with the mother persists unproblematically into adulthood. Whereas for men the degree to which they retain traces or indeed fixations stemming from the pre-oedipal level, when there was still an identification with the mother's body, creates fetishistic or paranoiac structures. The importance of the 19th century and early 20th century avant-garde work is partly to do with the way in which the identification with the mother, with the feminine, can be explored.

It is of the greatest political importance, however, to contest in this notion of the modern text—and therefore in my own reading of the Dreyer-text— the implicit idealist tendency to separate off artistic practices from other social and especially political practices. Without an *other* social-artistic practice, without *e.g.* a social practice of the cinema[18], Dreyer's films are as 'lost' as the copies of Joyce on the shelves of University bookshops. It is important to emphasise the social nature of this practice, not merely the assumption of the implicit anarchistic position towards the state and political action Kristeva correctly identifies as the dominant political tendency in avant-garde signifying practices.

II. 'I cannot talk about film without saying a couple of words about music. It is Heinrich Heine who has said that where the words come out short there the music begins' (Dreyer).
'But about the Professor there was music certainly; there was music in every syllable he uttered and there was music implicit in his name, the *Sieg-mund*, the victorious voice or utterance' (H.D.).

Let us return to *Day of Wrath* and the shadow on the sheet of music. There are several musical elements in the film, such as the dramatic opening music, which also accompanies Anne's visit to the church. Two musical elements dominate the film and are to some extent variations on a single theme: a) the *Dies Irae* itself, sung by a choir of 'angelic' young boys who thus give the music connotations of pre-pubertal innocence; and b) a more lyrical piece associated with Martin and Anne outdoors, walking, taking trips on the water (symbolic imagery already present in *The President* and *The Bride of Glomdale*), making love in the fields, which easily transforms into the more sinister *Dies Irae*-theme, *e.g.* in the scene where they encounter a cart loaded with fire-wood, foreshadowing the burning of the witch.

This image of the shadow cast on music which is written down, a semiotic process contained and constrained within the symbolic order of graphic notation, condenses meanings operative on a series of different levels. It highlights the symbolic/semiotic dialectic fundamental to artistic production, including the shadow-trace of the Master (*i.e.* the choir-master) literally conducting, organising and presiding over the tricky business of making sure the musical performance (dominated by the semiotic) remains within the bounds of the notation (dominated by the symbolic). As the Master, the agent of the law, whose mark of intervention (in this case: the shadow) constitutes the bar between semiotic/symbolic, he imprints the stamp of death, of stasis onto the flux of musical rhythm, doubling the connotation of death already inherent in the image of sheet-music, music frozen into an abstract pattern of notations. This doubling is re-inforced by a further mark of death: the title on the music, *Dies Irae*, being in the same script as the one used for writing the sentencing documents. At which point we are more explicitly referred to the real function of the Master as Sentencer, the one whose words signify death. That the music itself, the *Dies Irae* should be a hymn about the Last Judgement, rounds off and in a sense binds together all these various strands of meaning.

The connotations of pre-pubertal innocence, the repressed sexuality of the latency period, is marked by the boys' as yet unbroken voices. This 'feminine' pitch which can only be maintained into adulthood by that act of

23

feminisation which yet preserves an erstwhile culturally acceptable bisexuality, to which the body and the voice of the castrato bear witness (cf Barthes' *S/Z*). The feminine body is not allowed this ambivalence. Women's active expression of desire is read as witchcraft, punished by torture and burning. The pitch appropriate to a feminine bisexuality can be heard in the scream, the scream exactly that Anne hears *before we do* in the voices of the choirboys, translating their song as if she were singing it, from male dominated to female dominated bisexuality. Here we see the semiotic component of the voice differentially inflected by the symbolic order so that desire in the male can be sung, but in the female only when elided with death. When Anne reads from the *Song of Songs* (itself a lyric with bisexual connotations) she is stopped by her mother-in-law, who will denounce her and therefore send her to her death. A death, a dying that Barthes locates in the voice of the loved one: 'The fading of the other holds itself in her voice. The voice supports, makes visible and so to speak accomplishes the disappearance of the loved one because death belongs to the voice'[19]. The voice, as is the cinematic machine through which it is rematerialised for the spectator/listener, is marked by 'death at work'. The marks of death which according to Barthes constitute the modulation of the voice: 'This ghostly being of the voice, is its modulation. The modulation, defining characteristic of each voice, is that which is keeping silent, it is that grain of the voice which disintegrates and fades away'[19]. The voice can function similarly to the look and be the object or creation of a phantasy, equally ungraspable, present only in traces, always in the process of vanishing. This is supported in a general way in relation to the Dreyer-text by Dreyer's insistence on modulation as the final element in the profilmic event to be 'filled in'. More work is needed on the text in this area. For instance, it is likely that the sound track and in particular the musical scores, also play with absence, with silence. One of the effects so often referred to in relation to Dreyer is silence as an active value, silence produced from sound oppositions.

A. Téchiné writes: 'For at the heart of a system as rigorous as this, at the centre of so meticulous a structure, the least vibration figures as an uncertain gravitation, as an equilibrium disturbed and causing a divergence in the contours. The blink of an eyelid, a gesture by a hand, become irretrievable, because they incessantly elude the schematism that provokes and haunts them at every moment. Because they vaguely trace an élan one thought not possible here, and which is seen to persist, an outcropping on the surface of volumes'. This quotation accurately captures the value of semiotic interruptions, *e.g.* the movements when the voice 'cuts across' the song that is being sung, or the values created by a series of slight differences of camera position. The movement towards abstraction and 'minimalism' can also be understood in these terms. Not simply a repression, a putting out of sight, but a realisation that this interaction of symbolic and semiotic can occur whatever the number of elements present, and the pleasure of the 'least vibration' somehow resides in the minimal effort needed to produce it, a sense perhaps of an approach to a potential 'explosion' of the semiotic.

Work such as Kristeva's outlined earlier begins to pose the problems of the articulation of desire in a historical perspective. One indirect way in which semiotic excess finds expression has been described by Freud as conversion hysteria. The unaccommodated excess is somatised, appearing elsewhere, in the wrong place, transcribed into a different substance. For instance in the case of Dora[20] the patient felt the reverse of sexual stimulation, disgust, localised not in relation to the genital area, but in the mucous membrane of her throat. When it cannot receive direct genital expression, desire can be displaced onto other areas, other parts of the body thus become eroticised and their manipulation can give orgasmic satisfaction. These converted signifiers have an ideational content, they express repressed ideas through the medium of the body, and the Symbolic relation linking symptom and meaning is such that a single symptom may express several meanings either simultaneously or consecutively. Those symptoms which persist into the analytic situation take on a new sense in relation to the transference of affect onto the person of the analyst. This transferability of affect which forms the basis of psychoanalytic practice (and text construction) is that same 'suggestibility' isolated at the turn of the century by theoreticians of hypnosis but given wider theoretical and practical power by the elaboration of psychoanalysis.

In his essay *On Leaving the cinema*[21], R. Barthes comments on the similarity between the film viewing situation and that of the hypnotic scene: the pre-hypnotic situation of entering the cinema, the primary fantasy being that of becoming a spectator; the eroticisation of darkness; the immobile, but flickering light; and the sound and music which in Dreyer's films do not aid the effect of reality as Barthes suggests, but rather increase the suggestibility. Indeed Barthes recalls the healing use of music in hypnotic suggestion, and I think it is possible to see the music in Dreyer's films in this way, healing the fragmented body of the text. The Dreyer-text is particularly susceptible to analysis in terms of hypnosis as well as the more extended model of conversion hysteria. Not only does hypnosis emerge as a specific thematic concern in *Gertrud*, but many of the stylistic devices of the films have connotations of hypnosis. The emphasis on music, the modulation of the voice (the last element to be filled in by Dreyer in rehearsal), the slow pans, the light reflected off white walls back into the audience, the intense white light for flashbacks and rememoration in *Gertrud*, interiors lit with pools of light, characters moving into them to speak. Even critics have noted this apparent parallel with hypnosis: 'The audience forced into the illusion [of *Ordet*] is almost hypnotised' (Rasmussen)[22].

However, the relations of psychoanalysis and cinema do not rest there. Crude versions of psychoanalysis are an important element of some filmic contents, *e.g.* in Preminger and Hitchcock. The 'birth' of cinema is contemporaneous with that of psychoanalysis. Hypnosis has a privileged place in early cinema: *e.g. The Cabinet of Dr. Caligari*, the representations of the doctor with his thick spectacles and his gaze into camera, who *sees* into psychological (and supernatural) problems; Lang's *Dr. Mabuse*; the doctor in *Vampyr* where the result of the hypnosis is Gray's uncanny dream (central to vampirism) of lossing his own blood. Moreover, the diegesis of *Gertrud* is contemporaneous with the birth of psychoanalysis: Dr. Axel Nygren, her old friend who visits her at the same time that Gabriel Lidman returns, lives and works in Paris with a group who study psychology and psychiatry and experiment with hypnosis and telepathy. They discuss and argue about 'psychosis, neurosis, dreams and symbols', and they perform hypnotic experiments on an old woman. In fact, the theme of hypnosis can be read as a metaphor for the relation between Gertrud and the camera throughout the film.

In *Group Psychology and the analysis of the Ego*[23], Freud compares hypnosis with being in love but distinguishes it from that state by the absence of directly sexual trends. He continues: 'It contains an additional element of paralysis derived from the relation between someone with superior power [the hypnotist] and someone who is helpless [the patient], which may afford a transition to the hypnosis of fright which occurs in animals'. Hypnosis might be understood in terms of a particular identification of the scopic drive in such a way that the look itself becomes the (impossible) object of fascination. Is perhaps the paralysis of hypnosis which overtakes the spectator who looks at the Medusa's head, the paralysis of fear mitigated by the assurance of potency when 'becoming stiff' means an erection? The intensity of the subject's gaze at the hypnotist's little object which reflects light is conjoint with the hypnotist's gaze at the subject. The active exhibitionist component 'I am looking, I have a penis', copresent with the passive narcissistic component 'I am looked at and am therefore feminine'. The hypnotic state would then correspond to a certain vectoral balance, a bisexual positioning. Furthermore, what is also particular about hypnosis is the way the hypnotic subject does not speak, but is spoken. The representative of the subject, the 'I' is outside looking at the ego, the 'I' which voices but is not the speaking subject. In *Gertrud*, this 'I' speaks the language of the 'eternal feminine': the question from her lover Erland 'Who are you really?' (a version of the question Freud posed, 'What does woman want?') and the reply: 'I am the dew falling from the leaves and a white cloud passing overhead, going no one knows where . . . I am the moon, . . . I am the sky . . . I am a mouth seeking another mouth . . . it's like a dream, it is a dream . . . Life is a dream . . . a long succession of dreams which glide past one after the other'. In this dream-like state, the light flickering on her face, the desiring 'I' speaks Gertrud. Is not her body, spoken, the site of that framed discourse discussed in relation to *Michael?* There is the same problematisation of the system of address founding the cinematic institution: men/light, representatives of the subject of the discourse interrogate a 'you', the Gertrud who cannot enunciate, but only be enounced, spoken. She cannot speak ('I have not lived, no, but I have loved!') but is subject to the tyranny of being spoken, of being the passage through which desire enters the lives of others and around which she constructs a misrecognised identity.

It has been pointed out that critics comment on the experience of viewing a Dreyer film, its slowness, controlled rhythm, its silences, as being like hypnosis. Indeed special hypnoid viewing situations are created for the films. For the first run of *Ordet*, the projection booth was especially soundproofed to erase any trace of the sound of the projector (think also of the Anthology Film Archives in New York—which hold Dreyer high in their pantheon—, a cinema with all surfaces covered in non-reflecting black, each seat constructed like a medieval cell-like choir stall with one concession to sociality: the small incision through which people in adjacent seats may make hand contact. This cinema shifts the scopic drive towards the production of 'animal fright', terrorisation by the beam of light). The parallel of hypnosis with the viewer's position in the contemporary institution of cinema is evident: viewers are spoken as they follow the thread the story unwinds for them, they are not supposed to compose their own story line. They are addressed in that suggestible passivity, where one is sometimes forced to suspect the film of surreptitious sexual aggression (*e.g.* the debate about subliminal advertising; Tony Conrad's *Flicker*, etc). In the above mentioned essay, Barthes posed a mode of watching cinema, of a double fascination, as if one had two bodies at the same time, a narcissistic body 'lost in the mirror of the screen', and a 'perverse body' comprised of all that exceeds the screen , the sound, the room, the darkness, the obscure presence of others, the rays of light. If these fetishistic and narcissistic structurings of desire are abandoned, cancelled out, the subject then becomes prey to the light beam, as is Maria in *Metropolis*, terrorised by the beam of light, caught in a structure of looks in which she can have no libidinal investment.

'Amor Omnia—Love is everything', the tyranny of Gertrud's love has a material base: on marrying Kanning she is not allowed an independent life as a singer. Her doctrine of love can be read as the only outlet for her desire, her only way of retaining any autonomy. The film points to this problem in the scene where Kanning visits the opera hoping to find Gertrud. The attendant says he would have recognised her if she had been there that evening. On the wall is a poster of *Fidelio* (an opera with an ending connoting bisexuality). In the right hand side of the frame are two portraits, the larger of a man, the smaller of a woman, connoting the power relation: male dominance; and stating the problem: bisexuality. Both Gertrud's past and future are elided in the diegesis. Her time in Paris where she plays an active role, participating in the work of the study group, is not represented even though she renounces sexual relationships: she can work with Axel because they are not in love.

In the film, Gertrud sings two songs. The first is to the music of Erland Jansson's nocturne, the tune which also opens the film, and which recurs for instance in the sound of the church bells when she leaves her house for the last time, and in the music heard off-screen during the reception: 'Eternal and wingéd child and god/Once more I have heard your stern command/Once more my heart has obeyed/Once more I am lonely amid the satisfied crowd [camera moves to centre Gertrud and Erland at the piano with mirror behind]/Your burning severity will bring me sufficient happiness [exchange of looks, centering of frame]/Darkness has made a pearl/Night has created a dream/It shall live within me [camera returns L]/Dazzling white and tender/The song must sound within the heart/Painfully sweet and cruel/While my shining pearl grows within its dark surroundings' [Camera returns to original position]. This is a love song, but about love as pain, as suffering, opposed to Lidman's 'love without pain'. This concealed burning love is a product of a dream and of darkness. The *mise-en-scène* of the song is very precise, paralleling the movement of its sense towards intimacy, turning on the exchange of looks at line 5: a balancing movement such that the shot ends where it begins (one might speculate as to the medieval music framed on the wall, it might be Guillaume de Machaut's *My end is my beginning*), and within the shot a series of framings reinforcing the framing/reframing tension, which creates the 'static' quality of the film as a product of photography. The second song occurs following the reception, after Gertrud's old lover Gabriel Lidman reveals meeting her current lover Erland at a party, boasting of his conquest of her. The party is in fact the one Jansson, after sleeping with Gertrud, had promised he wouldn't attend. She sings: 'I feel no resentment, although my heart is broken/In the midst of my despair I see how you suffer/and I feel no resentment/Although your forehead is youthful and unlined/I know the heavy burden your heart must carry/I have known it for a long time/I feel no resentment, my friend now lost for ever'. At that point, she breaks down collapsing on the floor. The address of the song focusses the complexity of her situation. She is singing in front of all the men in her life: Kanning, Lidman, Jansson and Nygren. Jansson is separated from her by the piano, in opposition to the previous song at their first meeting where they were together at the keyboard. Facing them is the tapestry inscription of her dream: a woman attacked by hounds. The 'I' of the first line can refer to her, or Lidman who has just burst into tears. The 'you' can refer to all the men (except Axel) but also herself as addressed by an imagined other. Who does the song address? Who speaks? Her fainting reinforces the hysterical element of her headache brought on by the public appearance of her husband. It signifies the intensity of desire which can't be expressed even through the conjunction of words and music. The centrality of this dramatic scene with all the elements for expression apparently available, underlines the problem of her speech. A woman naked and vulnerable in her desire: 'I dreamt I ran naked through the streets, pursued by hounds', confronting these demanding men (they all want her back, misrecognising her). This is a nodal point of the film where the diegesis foregrounds the problem of address,—which 'I'?, which 'You'?, the framed discourses: the tapestry square on the wall, Gertrud framed by the arch in front of the piano, the structure of conversion hysteria diegeticised in her fainting.

Pictures in the diegesis operate an inner 'framed' discourse freezing desire into a series of marks, a representation, held only to be displaced by the movement of the narrative, by the next picture. This movement of frames follows a complex trajectory, reinforced by the interplay with other *objets d'art*, particularly mirrors. To isolate certain moments: firstly, Gertrud appears framed by double doors, behind her a Gainsborough-like portrait of femininity; later, parting from Lidman, they both sit under a Munch woodcut or engraving of a man and a woman looking separately out to sea, their backs to the viewer. Lidman sits under the man, Gertrud under the woman; finally over her desk at the cottage, a painting of pine trees, a cold early 20th century version of that genre to which Barthes' words *à propos* of Caspar David Friedrich apply: 'a desolate space which demands that I project myself there . . . forever abandoned . . . in need of maternal warmth'[24].

There is another poem in the film, not set to music, but spoken by the young leader of the welcoming group at the reception for Lidman. Addressing Lidman and the assembled guests, man to man (the women confined to waving scarves from the gallery), he recites: 'He never relinquished her lips/Ever deeper did they sink into one another/He felt as if he were journeying into space/A red star shone in the white haze of the moon/dimly at first, almost dying/then brighter and nearer it grew/became a flaming pool/He burned without pain/And the flames cooled his tongue like sharp wine'. It is clearly a masculine poem. The address is also made clear in the film: the young man speaks the poet's words while the poet listens as his words come back to him not quite recognising the self mirrored back. The address of the poem is equally clear: He never relinquished her lips—his to desire, hers to be desired. It presents a collection of romantic symbols, *e.g.* the loss of self in space, the red star of male desire in the white haze of the feminine moon, etc. The white haze, incidentally that is also the lighting convention for Gertrud's memories. And perhaps most importantly, it speaks of love without pain, *i.e.* without suffering, the opposite of that which characterises love for Gertrud. The youth continues with a speech: 'We discover infinity and eternity in sexual ecstasy. This is the greatness of your concept of eroticism. This is love without boundaries. For this love man was created and called upon'. In his reply, Lidman situates his romantic notion of love implicity in the past. He doesn't speak of eroticism, but of truth, the product of love and thought. Later Gertrud reminds him of other words he spoke and which he has long forgotten: 'I believe in the pleasures of the flesh and the irredeemable solitude of the soul', a more sensualist philosophy into which she herself is forced by his betrayal and the note she discovered on his desk: 'Women's love and man's work are enemies from the start'. With fame, Lidman has become 'cold as marble' and Gertrud now disputes his knowing anything about love: 'I saw that of all the men who became great, none knows or understands love, they look down on love. You have become one of them and I don't love you'. In this film the singing voice, the voice carried by music is the vehicle of the semiotic. Singing is the performance of desire, though ultimately blocked (her collapse). The male voice does not sing, its desire remains firmly within symbolic bounds, circumscribed by 'work', reduced by 'thought' to 'truth'. Men may make a career out of speaking about love, but they know nothing of it.

E. To summarise and conclude, it appears that the Dreyer-text can be characterised as a type of hysterical discourse [25]. This conclusion is based on the emergence of particular sets of representations at three different levels of the films: the diegesis, the *mise-en-scène* (*i.e.* the filmic writing) and the body of the text as unified segments.

a) *Diegesis:* a representation of the subject of the discourse is thrown into the diegesis, but caught up in the blocks and facilitations encountered, including, for instance, the flexibility of the literary models used. An analogy for this process of symptom formation might be that of a moving human shadow thrown over such uneven ground that it at times appears completely unrecognisable. In the case of the Dreyer-text, there is a whole series of such figures acting as the representative(s) of the organising instance, the authorial subject of the discourse: primarily idealised women and feminised men.

b) *Mise-en-scène:* the inscription of discharged emotion which cannot be accommodated within the action, subordinated as it is to the demands of family lineage and inheritance. It can only find representation in narrative dislocation, the loss of certainty as to whose point-of-view is being represented, and the displacement away from the inherent emotionality of the action, the 'burning character of the dramatic content', onto the *mise-en-scène* and music, 'the chaste form of photographic compositions' as the Danish critic Bjorn Rasmussen put it. As formal analyses of the Dreyer-text have shown (Burch, myself, Parrain), those breaks, that loss of certainty is organised as a system in the Dreyer-text, so much so that Parrain can state: 'The filmic writing of Dreyer is founded on the non-identification of spectator and character'[26]. In fact it is more a play with that non-identification, which has two aspects: a) the assertion of an authorial 'I' unmediated by character, unfictionalised; and b) the secondary revision, the Symbolic reinscribed into the text, systematising the breaks which, covered over in one place, appear elsewhere such as in the modulations of voice and music. Those qualities of immobility and abstraction often referred to as hallmarks of Dreyer's style, become, in this reading, symptoms which form part of the hysterical discourse, a kind of hysterical paralysis at the level of the *mise-en-scène*, a fictionalising pressure working through the diegesis pushing towards a resolution of the problems represented, against a counter-pressure tending to fixity, immobility. In *Gertrud* this vectoral balance may be said to be represented in the scenic tableaus. In *Ordet*, the economy is slightly different: a series of moving shots link the scenes, marking a process of exchange between town, church, farm and country, with these scenes as it were compensating for that mobility by their own immobility, with 270 degree pans, markedly more centred on the camera's axis. A fixity of movement all the more striking when compared to *Gertrud*.

30

c) *The body of the text*, the text as body itself marked, traversed by certain torsions, displacements, erotisations and symptom formations characteristic of conversion hysteria. At this level we are dealing with the phantasies which the filmic discourse 'as a whole' sets in play for the audience, independently of, or rather in addition to form and content. But we can also speculate on the significance of the act of filming as presented in/produced by the various texts. While the act of say oilpainting as self expression (*e.g.* Pollock *et. al.*) may be seen as essentially an anal activity, what are we to make of the processes of film production as it emerges from Dreyer's films? A number of Dreyer's procedures in the film-making process are worth commenting on from this perspective. Such as the tendency towards a 'rigid' organisation of the pro-filmic event, methodically going through a series of stages, filling in the action, movement, dialogue and finally the modulation of the voice, so that a successful take can be printed immediately and editing becomes merely a mechanical operation of assemblage completed in a few days. Moreover this is combined with the tendency towards ever longer takes minimising the elements to be assembled. The aesthetics of montage posed problems for Dreyer largely resolved by the introduction of sound. He wanted *Joan of Arc* to be a sound film because the *découpage* effected on the body of the film and representationally on Joan's body, demanded a reparation within the film in the form of music and the sound of the human voice. The reparation of the body in pieces not only restores narcissism, but reconstitutes the body of the mother from the infant's sadistic, punishing attacks[27]. If the fantasy of the body in pieces dominates in *Joan of Arc*, *Ordet* and *Gertrud* demonstrate different economies in which the body is both fragmented and reassembled, *i.e.* long takes bound together by music, a process duplicated at the diegetic level: in *Ordet* the reanimation of Inger's cut body, while *Gertrud* is cemented together by means of music. The body of Gertrud is continually framed, placed within an order from which she cannot escape, except through her hysteria and her singing voice in which her desire can surface (before being blocked by her marriage). The body of the mother re-assembled, 'maternal warmth' re-created as in the final phantasies of its resurrection: in *Ordet* this happens literally; in *Michael* it is represented by Zoret's smiling death under the cross and Michael comforted by the maternal Zamikow; in *Gertrud* 'the body disappears in the final absence of décor, where it exists as indication/trace' (Téchiné), the body of Gertrud merging with the body of the text, the visual surface of the film, the blank expanse of the door which dissolves into the blankness of end leader. The final scene in the cottage, which Dreyer added so that the audience would know that Gertrud 'had chosen solitude and accepted it[28]' is shot in whiter, more intense light, the same as the memories of her past with Erland Jansson and Gabriel Lidman. This final scene of old age is presented by means of the same conventions used for the inscription of the nostalgià for or the memory of the past from which she suffers but to which in the end she returns in that phantasy unity with the mother.

31

F. Postface

A note on the textual subject 'Dreyer' as commodity.
"The cinema's 'bad conscience' known as 'art cinema' " (John Ellis).

Much criticism of Dreyer's films has been a straightforward authorial cult, quite independently of the systems of signification of the films. Little attempt for instance has been made to relate Dreyer's style to 'his' earlier silent films. Much of this criticism purports to found itself on the alleged intentionality of the author, with the critic as some kind of privileged go-between, bolstering his/her claims for the cinema as the manifestation of authorial presence by his/her special access to the word and body of the director, as evidenced in interviews, the 'telling' anecdote or photograph indicating the physical proximity of critic and director. What is such criticism which talks of mastery, genius etc., other than the reinscription of the critic-subject's fantasy of being in the (incestuous) place of the son/daughter, 'at the feet of the master', etc? The notion of self expression at play in this discourse is, of course, hopelessly idealist. The textual subject 'Dreyer' is neither the biological individual, now dead, nor the totality of that individual's traces in the real, but the effect of a specific series of transformations, the result of a process of play with signification on the terrain where the cinematic institution and given social formations intersect. The work of the Dreyer-text within this institution is to foreground the phantasy structures at play in it, *i.e.* the way the institution structures phantasy. As such, the text can be read as foregrounding the problem of reading,[29] putting into play its coherence in ways which are open to progressive forms of reading. What is described as Dreyer's qualities, is in fact the result of inflections of more general phantasies basic to the institution as a whole and put into play, played with by 'Dreyer'. It is not insignificant that he should speak of the cinema as his only great passion. It is with the double sense of that term passion that this essay has concerned itself. The active and passive, bisexual positioning implied by the words: passion = love, masculinity; and passion = suffering, feminity. Positions which each of us constantly traverses in our own history, which includes that history of encounters with cinematic texts and the processes of producing/being produced by them.

Carl Dreyer worked in most of the major European production centres of his time and with a number of different production companies. He took no interest in the financing of his films, nor in box office returns,[30] with the result that the rights to his films are held by various companies and individuals whose interests are more likely to be obtaining the best return on capital rather than any altruistic exhibition of his films in complete prints of good quality. One of the production companies, Palladium, allowed distribution rights to lapse on the films they held, for reasons that are not altogether clear. Perhaps, as one of Denmark's more successful producers of porno films, they did not regard Dreyer as a continuing commmercial proposition. In any event the films have recently appeared in this country, some of them in rather grey, worn prints, refugees from the American distribution market, and since one of the major pleasures of Dreyer films is precisely dependent on the light values, the use of delicate shades of grey, of high and low contrast lighting and photography, it is a particularly painful experience to have to witness this new mutilation of the body of the text in the name of profitability. The case of *Vampyr* is slightly different. True, the print in distribution in this country is a particularly mutilated version of the original, such that at points its system becomes completely opaque, but the main reason for its absence from our screens is due to wrangles over copyright.

I doubt, however, if there is still a future for Dreyer's films in the straight commercial distribution. Their successes have tended to be *succès d'estime* rather than financial successes. Journalists have always been divided: Dreyer's films are a point of contention, a scene for struggle, which can become extremely abusive (for example the première of *Gertrud* in Paris, where despite or perhaps because of his great critical standing with magazines like *Cahiers du Cinéma*, journalists refused to take the film seriously and vilified it in the press)[31]. In a sense, the problem is quite simple. Compared with other 'art films', Dreyer's films are too 'boring', they make too many demands on the spectator, they resist passive consumption, a degree of mobility is required for the inscribed reader that audiences find difficult to adopt because of the long and vigorous rule of journalistic models of reading terroristically imposed and maintained by the industry as well as cultural institutions such as film theatres, magazines, etc.

The production systems within which Dreyer worked were resistant to his way of film making particularly to his demand for total control. A legal battle with Société Generale apparently resulted in a reputation for not bringing films in within their budgets, the effect was that he had to serve a second apprenticeship in documentary film-making before being offered another contract he felt able to accept, *i.e. Day of Wrath*. Otherwise, Dreyer rejected all contracts, such as the one with Film Traders for the production of *Mary Stuart*, which didn't give him total artistic control. He preferred not to make films rather than compromise, and this hatred of compromise shows, I think, in his over-reaction against *Two People*. But apart from *Vampyr*, which was financed independently, and his short films, which were state financed, Dreyer was funded as everyone else, because he was expected to bring some return on the investment. Moreover the commercial situation in which his films were placed benefited from critical elaborations in terms of art, which in turn reacted back on the kinds of projects financed. Towards the end of his life the Danish State subsidised Dreyer by giving him the license of a cinema, the Dagmar in the centre of Copenhagen, where he apparently only showed films he liked. It was his own personal 'art house'.

The extension of the notion of 'art cinema' to cover an element of European production, is in need of a more theoretically coherent articulation of the apparatuses of production, distribution and exhibition at a nation state as well as European level (if indeed these are the relevant unities) and the ideologies with which they intersect. The notion of a European culture within which the Dreyer-text is placed is obviously an ideological one. The notion of a Scandinavian cultural placing has more substance in that most of the source materials for the films are drawn from the Danish linguistic formation (Danish is intelligible to Norwegians and Swedes, and was hegemonic in Norway until the 1930s), which gives it some unity at the literary level as well. This work has yet to be done, difficult as it is since any such reconstruction is also 'a construction in the present, for today' (Stephen Heath)[32]. Therefore, we should be clear about the kinds of questions we want to ask in the present. Hopefully, the following dossier as well as my own notes may contribute towards the formulation of such questions.

Notes

1. For a discussion of the problem of suture, see Stephen Heath, *Screen*, vol. 17 nr. 3; Claire Johnston, *Edinburgh Magazine '76*, nr. 1; J. A. Miller, J. P. Oudart, Stephen Heath, *Screen*, vol. 18, forthcoming issue.
2. Stephen Heath, *Screen*, vol. 17 nr. 4.
3. Ibid.; the quote within S.H.'s argument stems from Lacan, *Le Séminaire*, vol. XI.
4. See my essay on *Vampyr* in *Screen*, vol. 17 nr. 3. The structure of uncertainty, as the essay argues at some length, refers to T. Todorov's definition of the fantastic in relation to the shots of David Gray in the coffin, depicted with open eyes whereas he is supposed to be dead. The film in fact plays on this 'uncertainty' throughout its text.
5. R. Barthes, *Fragments d'un Discours Amoureux*, Paris 1977.
6. Paul Willemen, 'The Fugitive Subject' in *Raoul Walsh*, Edinburgh 1974.
7. *Jacques Tourneur*, Edinburgh 1975.
8. *Raoul Walsh*, Edinburgh 1974.
9. *Screen*, vol. 17 nr. 3. See also the remarks on point-of-view structures in David Bordwell's *Filmguide to La Passion de Jeanne d' Arc*, Bloomington 1973.
10. Both quotations from Foucault's *The Order of Things*, London 1970.
11. Other determinants for this drift towards semantic structures turning on religious notions were mentioned earlier in this essay. The overall implication of these notes is that 'religion' as a thematic nexus is overdetermined by different processes at work in the very fabric of the texts. If a dominant determining process must be identified, it would appear to me that the arguments put forward in relation to the 'light' as the signifier of the structuring phantasy of the Dreyer-text, are the decisive ones.
12. R. Barthes, op. cit.
13. Little of Julia Kristeva's work is available in English. In the present context, I will be referring primarily to her essay *Signifying Practice and Mode of Production*, published in the *Edinburgh Magazine '76*, nr. 1.
14. There are no children in Dreyer's films!
15. Kristeva, op. cit.
16. See *e.g.* Edward Carpenter's discussion of these issues in *Love's Coming of Age*, London, first published 1896, 12th edition 1923. The terminology is Carpenter's.
17. Interview with J.K., *Substance*, nr. 13, Madison 1976.
18. For the concept 'social practice of cinema', see C. Johnston and P. Willemen, *Brecht in Britain—The Independent Political Film* in *Screen*, vol. 16, nr. 4, and C. Johnston, *Notes on the Idea of an Independent Cinema*, unpublished SEFT—seminar paper (1977), which contains some valuable correctives to the former essay.

19. R. Barthes, op. cit.
20. S. Freud, *Standard Edition*, vol. VII.
21. In *Communications*, nr. 19.
22. In *Catholica*, nr. 1, 1955.
23. S. Freud, *Standard Edition*, vol. XVIII.
24. R. Barthes, *Fragments d'un Discours Amoureux*, Paris 1977.
25. Geoffrey Nowell-Smith, 'Minnelli and Melodrama' in *Screen*, vol. 18 nr. 2, offers some interesting comments on the nature of the hysterical text.
26. In *Etudes Cinématographiques*, nr. 53/56.
27. Incidentally, this hypothesis casts a new light on the Bazinian arguments in favour of realism. Regarding the phantasy of 'the body in pieces': 'This fragmented body, the term for which I have introduced into our theoretical frame of reference, regularly manifests itself in dreams when the movement of analysis encounters a certain level of agressive disintegration in the individual. It then appears in the form of disjointed limbs, or of those organs figured in exoscopy, growing wings and taking up arms for intestinal persecutions . . . but this form is even more tangibly revealed at the organic level, in the lines of 'fragilisation' which define the anatomy of phantasy, as exhibited in the schizoid and spasmodic symptoms of hysteria'. J. Lacan, 'The Mirror Phase' in *New Left Review*, nr. 51.
28. Dreyer in an interview in *Film Comment*, vol. IV nr. 1.
29. See Paul Willemen's remarks about the categorisation of textual systems in his essay in *Jacques Tourneur*, Edinburgh 1975.
30. This is stated in a letter from Ib Monty to Ernest Lindgren of 20.9.65.
31. See the report on this distasteful occasion in *Cahiers du Cinéma*, nr. 207.
32. *Edinburgh Magazine 1977*.

III. Dreyer Dossier

Apart from the basic filmographic information, the material in this section has been chosen because it complements the theses outlined in my article, and also to suggest points of entry to that piece starting from the individual films. Except where indicated, all quotes are from *Cahiers de Cinéma,* particularly their special issue on Dreyer (nr. 207, Dec. 1968). At times *Cahiers'* remarks about the films come very close to the position I have tried to develop in my essay.

It is interesting to speculate on the reasons why *Cahiers du Cinéma* produced this type of analysis of Dreyer's work shortly after the events of '68, which were characterised by, amongst other things, a massive politicisation of cultural and particularly aesthetic practices. *Cahiers'* focus on the problems of language and subjectivity combined with an almost total absence of any attempt to theorise these problems within a materialist framework, may well be symptomatic of some serious shortcomings inherent in the ideologies which helped to produce and dominated the progressive cultural practices accompanying May '68. In fact, it was not until the early 70s that *Cahiers'* vanguard position, somewhat idealist in this respect, began to be rectified.

A. Biography

Born: February 3rd 1889—Died: March 20th 1968.
His Swedish mother died soon after he was born and he was adopted by a Danish family. He was given piano lessons and got a job as a pianist in a cafe. However, it lasted only for one evening. After working in various offices, he became a journalist writing theatre reviews for small provincial papers. Subsequently, he worked for three influential papers in Copenhagen, *e.g.* he was the Air Sports correspondent for the *Belingske Tidende*, and became an active member of the University Student's Club. Among his journalistic duties for the *Extrabladet* was the writing of a series of satires called *Heroes of our Time* under the pseudonym Tommen.

In 1912, he joined the Nordisk Films Kompagni as dialogue writer, soon graduating to scriptwriter. He adapted novels acquired by the studio at his suggestion, such as Rousthoj's *Hotel Paradis*, filmed in 1917. In 1918, having worked in every department of film making, he asked to direct his adaptation of K. E. Franzo's novel *The President*. The film was released in 1919.

After making *Vampyr*, Dreyer apparently came to Great Britain to work with Grierson and the documentary film makers. At one point, he went to North Africa to prepare a film about a white man 'going native', but this project was abandoned by the producers. For several years he continued his journalistic activities, writing reports from the law courts under his old pseudonym Tommen. He recommenced directing in 1942.

When *Cahiers du Cinéma* asked Dreyer about his early years, he commented:

> 'I did a few reviews, a little theatre criticism but mostly I covered trials. Every day I gave a complete account of what had happened at the Court House. This work also gave me the opportunity of studying many middle class personalities. It was as a theatre critic that I saw the play from which *Day of Wrath* was taken. It was in this way as well that I saw *Ordet*, out of which I was to make a film in 1954. I also did a little cinema criticism. There was also a period during which I worked in journalism in the mornings and the cinema in the afternoon. I began in the cinema by doing titles for silent films. At that time, Nordisk was making about a hundred films a year. There were five or six directors who worked the four summer months and who did not edit their films themselves. They sent them to the laboratory. Well, that's where I was, together with someone who was the director of the laboratory. We worked together, and put in the necessary texts. This was a genre of work that constituted a marvelous school. Following that, I wrote some scenarios and then I began to film novels. But before that I "went to school" for five years. Today, when I work, the film edits itself in my head, gradually, during the shooting. It is part of the *mise-en-scene*.'

B. Filmography

1919 Praesidenten
(The President)

Production	Nordisk Films Kompagni (Copenhagen)
Script	Dreyer. Based on the novel by Karl Emil Franzos.
Director of Photography	Hans Vaagø
Art Director	Dreyer

Halvard Hoff (*Karl Victor von Sendlingen, the President*), Elith Pio (*his father*), Carl Meyer (*his grandfather*), Olga Raphael-Linden (*Victorine Lippert, his daughter*), Betty Kirkebye (*Hermine Lippert*), Richard Christensen (*Lawyer Georg Berger*), Peter Nielsen (*prosecutor*), Axel Madsden (*Vice-President Werner*), Hallander Hellemann (*Franz*), Fanny Petersen (*Brigitta*), Jacoba Jessen (*Maika*), Jon Iversen (*Victorine's fiancé*).
Length: 1700 m.

Dreyer introduced a more naturalistic style into the staple Nordisk melodrama, insisting on building his own scenery and using non-professional actors:

> 'I made this film somewhat as a study and for the experience. What was pleasing to me was the flashback, which at that time was something new. But even then I was beginning to do my own décors, and I also tried to simplify them. As for the actors, at that time there were very few. There were, notably, at Nordisk, two or three actors who absolutely played all the parts that called for old people, who specialised in it and who were always called whenever you needed someone old. For the first time, I took, to play old people, *old* men and *old* women. Today, this is a completely normal thing but at that time I was breaking with a tradition. I also took, for bit parts, instead of certain other actors who were proposed to me, people I met on the street. I chose two second rank actors as well, who were better than the famous but routine actors who were offered to me.'

The approach used here was suggested in part by a question posed by Laura Mulvey at a SEFT* weekend school as to the mechanisms in films such as Dreyer's and Sirk's which enable the foregrounding of the problem of representing woman's desire, a problem central to *All that Heaven Allows* for example. Although this question is more productively pursued in relation to Dreyer's later films, such as *Gertrud*, the conventions of melodrama are also central to this first film.

The President is a film literally dominated by the novel (the film as novel, the filmed novel). We see its opening and closing pages, the title page giving the title (The

President of the Court), author (A novel by Karl Emil Franzos) and place of publication (Copenhagen), with 'Nordisk Films' as the publisher. Then we see Karl Victor's asymmetrical family tree, followed by the credit 'adapted for film and directed by Carl Th. Dreyer'. The film tells of a particular constellation of familial and class relations common to much 19th century melodramatic literature and theatre.

Aware that he is dying, Franz Victor writes in his diary that that very day his son Karl Victor shall learn the wrongs he, Franz Victor, has comitted against the family. In a flashback sequence, set in the ruins of the family estate he confesses to his son how he once fell for a gamekeeper's daughter who 'bewitched' him. He had refused to marry her when she was pregnant, but she wrote to his father, who forced him to marry her with the words: 'A von Sendlingen can be a rake, but not a scoundrel'. Franz Victor gets his son to swear, over a fallen family crest among the ruins, that he will never repeat his father's mistake: 'Never make any common girl your wife, because no good will come of it, only a curse for the both of you, a curse and remorse'.

From the very beginning, the terms of melodrama have been introduced: the family problem, the inheritance, tradition, the family's ruination because of an interclass marriage. In fact, the ruination is quite literally represented by decayed property, as the intertitle states: 'The once proud castle is now a playground for the children of the poor'. The son's oath then commits him to retain property relations intact by restraining his sexuality. The problem of generations is reinforced in the opening shots by the tracery of ancestral cameos covering walls of Karl Victor's house, as they are contrasted with austere walls of the servants' quarters. Indeed the lower classes are not supposed to have a history as history = property. Sexuality is split into desire (aristocratic, symbolised by idyllic images of water) and procreation (evil, symbolised by the intercutting of shots of the children of the poor with images of toads). At this stage, mothers do not appear to exist, only fathers and children. The only 'mother' on the scene is referred to as the gamekeeper's daughter.

Thirty years later, Karl Victor is a successful lawyer, 'the town's honoured and loved President of the Court' who carries out his duties in accordance with the family motto: The majesty of justice is the most holy thing on earth. Returning from an official journey, he looks over the documents of an impending trial of a woman, Victorine Lippert, for infanticide. From another letter he learns that the alleged murderess is his daughter, named after him by the mother whom he has (presumably) abandoned. He confesses this to his deputy Berger and the circumstances of the affair are shown in flashback. He fell in love with the governess of his uncle's daughter (they are seen on a bridge, kissing, with water below). Quoting his grandfather, he resolves to marry her, but being reminded of his oath to his father he deserts her. Returning to the diegetic present, Karl Victor requests his deputy to take over the case.

In the trial, Victorine's story is spoken by the defence counsel (again depicted in flashback). On the death of her mother, who was a governess, the 17 year old Victorine also takes a post as a governess with a Countess. She becomes involved with the countess's son, who promises to marry her when he returns from a voyage he is about to make. She writes to him about her pregnancy, but receives no reply. Instead he writes to his mother suggesting Victorine is equally to blame for the unfortunate affair. Victorine is immediately expelled still in her nightdress. A dog chases her off the estate. The next morning she is found unconscious with her dead child beside her. In the diegesis, the eviction, the birth and death of the child are all collapsed into one another. It would perhaps be an understatement to say that something is repeating itself! The play on law and more precisely patriarchal law, is also clear. Moreover, in a court of (patriarchal-bourgeois) law, women have no voice: Victorine does not speak, she—her story and defence—is spoken by her lawyer.

The death sentence is pronounced. Her father, the President asks his deputy Berger to prepare Victorine for his visit. Her reaction to this is presented in the film as three uncommented tableaus: one of her mother's death, then a shot of herself in mourning, and finally we see her reading a letter (yet another letter) from her mother which says: 'Should fate ever take you to your father, then tell him that I have forgiven him'. These memory scenes are presented in static, frozen tableaux. Father and daughter are then reunited in best melodramatic fashion. Her father, the President, says he'll try for a reprieve, adding: 'Thank God I am álive to repay my debt'. A letter (sic) arrives communicating his advancement to President of the Provincial Court, and this enables him to avoid carrying out the death sentence on Victorine, *i.e.* he will no longer be tempted to break the law for having to enforce it. He lies to his daughter informing her that the appeal has been successful. He has to go to a farewell ceremony in his honour (with a spectacular torchlight parade), but still feels tormented. Eventually he withdraws from the party, gets Victorine out of her cell and bundles her off in a coach. He writes a letter(!) of resignation claiming failing health and departs by train, as if nothing had happened. At a certain point in their journeys, the paths of train and coach cross. Von Sendlingen secretly joins the coach and drives across the border.

Three years later. On a journey abroad, on board a river steamer, advocate Berger meets a plantation owner from Java, who has come to Europe to get married. Berger recognises the picture of the wife to be as that of Victorine. There is a hastily arranged marriage (complete with blind organist) and the couple return to Java. Parallel to this is the domestic business of preparing the return home prefaced by a bizarre scene in which one of von Sendlingen's servants completes a memorial to a recently dead cat, watched by three dogs, who then observe the wedding ceremony from the back pew of the church, and follow the bride into the carriage. These animals were introduced as puppies and kittens earlier in the diegesis, and so serve to mark the passing of time, as well as marking the loss (the death of the cat) of the daughter.

Returning home, Karl Victor admits his 'crime' to the new President: 'I have come to ask for the punishment due to me as a criminal'. However the new President responds to this confession with the words: 'What you have told me here must remain a secret. If it becomes known it will completely destroy respect for the judiciary'. When Karl Victor then threatens to accuse himself publicly, the new incarnation of the Law, Werner, threatens to find and arrest his daughter and carry out the death penalty. Bowing to the will of Werner, Karl Victor writes his testament and returns, past the old gallows' place, to the ruins of his forefathers' castle. On top of the same wall below which he walkéd with his father, he slips or jumps. Then follows a final shot of an hour glass that has run out and the book closes with an inscription to Karl Victor: 'Honoured be his memory'.

As is predominantly the case in Dreyer's films up to *Joan of Arc*, the viewer is placed in the privileged position of knowledge, characteristic of most 19th century fiction. Point-of-view structures or subjective shots are not present in the film. The time relations in the film read as a transposition from the novel rather than as anything specifically cinematic. Titles are invariably used to indicate the time, except for the detail of the ageing of the domestic animals already mentioned. The film generally presents a surplus of signification, not structured overdetermination as in

40

the decor of *Michael*, but simply excess, with long titles fixing the meaning of the scenes. However the main source of this excess is to be found in the obsessive repetition of structure which itself presents one of the main characteristics of desire: the compulsion to repeat.

Perhaps the most striking feature of the film is the insistence of letters. Usually the motors of narrative action, sometimes duplicating it, they are almost invariably written by men and addressed to men. This is perhaps not surprising in a diegesis dominated by male characters, but it connects with the general refusal to give women a voice in the film. Hermine, Victorine's mother, is said to have written to the Countess' son, but this letter is not shown. Hermine does write to Victorine, saying she has forgiven Karl Victor, but this letter is marked as different by the 'memories' it evokes in Victorine: whereas 'male' letters provoke or explain actions, Victorine's memories are frozen tableaux, almost alien inserts into the fiction. The legal correspondence accounts for about half of the letters in the film but they also underscore the male discourse as the agent of the patriarchal Law organising sexuality.

At the end of the film the 'once proud family' is still 'in ruins'. The ruins remain, as Karl Victor has not been able to confess. There is no resolution to the conflicts other than his (childless) death. To have had his confession accepted, would have marked his return to the letter of his grandfather's edict (which decreed that if one gets a girl pregnant, one must marry her) and his actions would have become once more legally recognised and codified. In fact the grandfather's words constitute a compromise: they permit marriage across class boundaries, privileging the maintenance of the family as the only place for sexuality, overriding considerations of property. The father's injunction never to marry a common woman represents the more uncompromising position of rampant virility presented by the film as self contradictory. By contradicting the grandfather's edict, it is itself in violation of the Law. Karl Victor's father, of course, did exactly what he forbids his son, and so his successfully socialised son is destined to disobey him. Bearer of the law (as Judge), he must also break the law. To resolve this dilemma, all that is left is death, whereupon the 'problem' can be evacuated from the fiction. Victorine is packed off to Java.

*   *   *

1919 Blade af Satans Bog

(Leaves from Satan's Book)

Production	Nordisk Films Kompagni
Script	Edgar Høyer, Dreyer. Based on the novel *The Sorrows of Satan* by Marie Corelli.
Director of Photography	George Schnéevoigt
Art Director	Dreyer, with technical assistance by Axel Bruun, Jens G. Lind.

Helge Nissen (*Satan*). *First episode:* Halvard Hoff (*Jesus*), Jacob Texiere (*Judas*), Erling Hansson (*John*), Wilhelm Jensen (*Carpenter*). *Second episode:* Hallander Hellemann (*Don Gomez*), Ebon Strandin (*Isabella*), Johannes Meyer (*Don Fernandez*), Nalle Halden (*The Majordomo*), Hugo Bruun (*Count Manuel*). *Third episode:* Tenna Kraft (*Marie Antoinette*), Emma Wiehe (*The Countess of Chambord*), Jeanne Tramcourt (*Geneviève*), Elith Pio (*Joseph*), Viggo Wiehe (*Count of Chambord*), Emil Helsengreen (*The People's Commissar*), Sven Scholander

41

(*Michonnet*), Viggo Lindstrøm (*Père Pitou*), Vilhelm Petersen (*Fouquier-Tinville*). *Fourth episode:* Carlo Wieth (*Paavo*), Clara Pontoppidan (*Siri*), Carl Hillebrandt (*Rautaniemi*), Karina Bell (*Naima*), Christian Nielsen (*Corporal Matti*). Length: 3254 m.

Explaining that he had conceived the Christ-episode as a kind of 'iconographic image', he told *Cahiers du Cinéma* that his favourite episode was the last one:

Dreyer: It was there that, for the first time, I used a close up of the principal actress, in which she did what I asked of her and rendered a whole range of feeling, with a long succession of changing expressions.

CdC: In the Finnish episode, we find one of those young women who appear constantly in your films and around whom it seems your work is organised.

D: It wasn't wilful. Each time, it was the subject that attracted me. Here in this Finnish story, the subject pleased me very much: the story of a woman who sacrifices her life for her husband and her country, in spite of everything that rises against her and the threat of her children being killed. In the end she commits suicide.

CdC: In your first films montage is very important.

D: Very much so. The modern section was I think 750 metres in length, in which there were 600 shots. It was rapid montage. (But) it just came out like that, I didn't do it intentionally, there just were a great many movements and actions in that section.

CdC: Were you not influenced by theories of montage?

D: No. Although I'd just seen *Intolerance*. It was possible that I'd been influenced by that . . .

CdC: Did you yourself have any theory of montage, regarding your work, then or later?

D: No . . .

CdC: Certain filmmakers are also theorists. Are you in any way one of them?

D: No. I follow my inspiration. The secret is inspiration during shooting, during the editing . . . While shooting, one is already editing, one has already done the editing, mentally. If I do a number of shots today, I will edit them during the night, and if I notice that the montage would be better with a close-up, then I will shoot the close-up tomorrow while the set is still there . . . [*Leaves from Satan's Book* and *Joan of Arc* both] have white walls. I have always loved white walls and I use them in nearly all my films. Even the last act of *Ordet* was against a white background.

J. L. Comolli described the film in the following terms:

'As early as 1920, almost the whole of Dreyer's *oeuvre* seems to be contained within the four episodes of his second film, summarised or rather sketched in outline. Here the threads used in weaving that *oeuvre*, few in number, making them all the easier to pick out, are already in position. Though barely removed from the conventions of the Film d'Art, *In Palestine* (or *The Passion of Jesus Christ*) is a first (emphatic) intimation of the *Jesus of Nazareth* that was so often projected and invariably postponed.

But it is with *The Red Rose of Finland* that one attains the essence of Dreyer's work, and Siri is justly placed alongside Anne, Inger or Gertrud as one of the great Dreyerian heroines.

Yet aside from this figure of a loving woman, she too a sacrifice, and aside from this very theme of sacrifice, of resistance to any intolerance or violence (the theme of the entire film, which the later works were of course to develop), there is nothing to remind one of the more familiar Dreyer. Just as *The Parson's Widow* simultaneously reveals and consummates what must be described as the comedy in Dreyer's work (a comedy, or rather a mocking irony, first given free rein in his humorous-moralistic reports and sketches as a journalist, and running like a watermark through his work, long masked by the extreme solemnity of the subjects, repressed in the interests of stringency and austerity, and unexpectedly reappearing in more than one scene in *Ordet* as well as in Gertrud's view of men and of the vanities that fetter her), so *The Red Rose of Finland* opens and closes the 'adventure film' chapter in Dreyer's *oeuvre*. But for the Finnish snows and forests in which its chases take place, this episode would in fact be a perfect Western no less than those of Ince or Hart (though of course Stiller, with the same not too important reservation, was also a master of the Western). Nothing else is missing, really: the lonely cabin in the woods, the telegraph station, a woman between two men, the good guys and the bad guys, innocent or guilty, fair or foul in the best tradition. Not to mention all the cavalry pursuits, the gunplay, the dramatic reversals, the boundless courage and the worst of intentions, the heroic or heinous actions. And here is this film-maker who might (at first glance) seem to be confined to a more limited focus, bounded by close-ups and dedicated to subtly caressing movements, now letting himself go, organising fights, on the trail of galloping horses, expanding his frame to take in hills and rivers (yielding in passing some wonderful—perhaps all the more so for being so out of character—scenes 'of nature').

Though a Western, however, it is not without its politics: the good guys are of course the innocent Whites, and the bad guys are the Reds. The peaceable telegraph operator, betrayed by his 'brother' who vainly loves Siri, is delivered by him into the hands of the Communists but saved by the reactionaries. And the leader of the Reds is the selfsame Satan who, in the three preceding episodes, had spun the webs of temptation and recantation. One should probably not conclude too hastily from this that Dreyer, scarcely conversant with political ideas, had yielded to his class prejudices, thus proving himself a reactionary. His hatred of the bourgeoisie and of all the repressions it has imposed in the name of religion or morality is well known. What then is the reason for this curious alliance, seemingly aggravated by the French Revolution episode, in which Satan assumes the mask of a people's commissar in order to bring apparently innocent aristocrats to perdition? Two explanations may be put forward: the first, perhaps a little too simple, is that Dreyer always takes the side of the weak and the oppressed against the oppressors, no matter what camp they belong to. The second is that for Dreyer oppression, with its manifestations of intolerance or violence, is all the more to be condemned and the more strongly denounced in that it stems from those who are supposedly responsible for justice, in that it is the stigma besetting good causes, and here one is reminded of Paulhan's *Lettre aux Directeurs de la Résistance:* 'It is worse that the Inquisition should be conducted in the name of God, the Terror in the name of Equity, the Repression in the name of the Revolution'. A certain gradation in the means employed by Satan to incite his agents to treachery in *Leaves from Satan's Book* may perhaps support this argument. A few pieces of silver suffice for Judas to betray Jesus; but the ruling class is corrupt, itself treacherous, and Jesus passes for something of a revolutionary. Next it is the jealousy inspired equally by his fortune, his daughter and his knowledge that is the astrologer's undoing, placing him in the hands of the Inquisition. Then, nothing but love and desire can serve the Devil's interests: for love the valet betrays his masters, and for the same reason Siri dies. As if, concurrently with changes in the nature of the societies depicted, the motivations for betrayal had shifted from a political and social plane (the alliance of Judas, the Romans and the Pharisees against Jesus; the conspiracy of the Church, but also of eminent citizens, against the power and knowledge of the astrologer) to a wholly personal one: nothing can be taken from the aristocrats, already dispossessed and destitute, but honour and love; nothing can be taken from Siri and her husband except simply their happiness. It is probable that Jesus would have been betrayed and the astrologer burned even had Satan not taken a hand; but his intervention with the French revolutionaries and the Bolsheviks had to be in order that, before being *torn** from it—and thereby exorcised!—these last two pages (being *pages of history*) should figure in his Book.'

Critics always compare this film, to its detriment, with D. W. Griffith's *Intolerance*. Dreyer admits being influenced by the film, but despite the thematic similarity with Griffith's film (which one might characterise as naïve/reactionary versions of history and historical change), it has none of the structural radicalism of *Intolerance*. The episodes of Dreyer's film are presented sequentially, and in chronological order, as opposed to Griffith's alternating syntagmatic structure. Technically one could point to 'advances' on his work in *President*, such as the use of masks, camera movement, POV structures to direct attention, close-ups, the gradual mastery of narrative montage within the episodes as the film progresses, etc. Our present concern is with a particular area of the film's work: the intersection of its presentation of history with that of desire. The episodes represent a series of social forces through the conflicts between the protagonists, broadly treated in terms of religion: the Jews versus a heretic religion, *i.e.* Jesus; the Counter-Reformation and the heretic New Science; the false religion of the Republic and the false religion of Communism.

Following the conventions of early 19th century melodrama, a series of libidinal struggles encouraged by Satan intersect with these 'historical' concerns; and the object of masculine desire is 'naturally' an abjectly suffering woman (or Jesus . . .). The major female protagonists and Jesus are all sacrificed or sacrifice themselves: Jesus anticipates and accepts his betrayal (a parallel that later *Michael* will draw on); Isabella is burnt after being raped by a member of the Inquisition; Geneviève is not raped, but betrayed to the republic's officers because she resists. Her mother by refusing to lie, and Marie-Antionette, by refusing to take orders, condemn themselves to death; Siri commits suicide, rather than be raped. It is easy to see how Jesus fits into this series of exemplary sufferers.

Male desire initially located outside of institutions, has to be harnessed to them (the Jewish Law, the Jacobin Club, the Inquisition, the Red Army) by means of the promised reward of eventual sexual gratification. Such desire is however presented as basically evil (it is encouraged by Satan) and there is no question of a mutual attraction or indeed of women even having any desire at all. And in true patriarchal fashion, access to the women involves removing them from their familial attachments.

*   *   *

*One of several titles used for this film in France is *Pages arrachées au livre de Satan* (Leaves Torn from Satan's Book) [Transl. Note].

1920 Prästänkan

(The Parsons's Widow/The Fourth Marriage of Dame Margaret/Youth to Youth)
Production   Svensk Filmindustri (Stockholm)
Script   Dreyer. Based on a short story by Kristofer Janson.
Director of Photography George Schnéevoigt

Hildur Carlberg (*Margarete Pedersdotter*), Einar Rød (*Söfren*), Greta Almroth (*Mari*), Olav Aukrust and Kurt Welin (*The aspiring pastors*), Mathilde Nielson (*Gunvor*), Emil Helsengreen (*The Gardener*), Lorentz Thyholt (*The Beadle*). Length: 1500 m.

At the time of its release in Britain (1921) even *Kine Weekly*, a publication not noted for its perceptive remarks or critical positions, gave the film a publicity boost. Commenting on its comedy qualities, its pastoral appeal and qualifying the whole as 'a work of artistic genius', the review went on: 'There can be little doubt that *Youth to Youth* will prove an exceptionally strong attraction both for those who look to the screen for sheer entertainment and for those who appreciate it as one of the fine arts'. (*K.W.*, 21/4/21.)

Sylvie Pierre was more coherent:

'Probably the Dreyer film in which the theme of female supremacy is most clearly stated . . . Rarely has more ferocious malice at the expense of the male been exercised in the cinema. Vainly trying to escape the matriarchal vigilance of his wife in a pathetically obvious adulterous affair (he introduces his mistress into the house as his sister), the young pastor suffers every conceivable obstruction, indignity and humiliation while the moral and aesthetic—and therefore poetic—stature of Dame Margaret steadily increases. One is reminded of *The Golden Coach* and the Viceroy who is "too small" compared to Magnani. An interplay of pettiness and generosity, of greatness and smallness, that constitutes one of the finest films ever constructed on the mechanisms of subterfuge and openness, of mendacity and its discomfiture, of the tangled circumnavigations of guilt and the straight course of rectitude. The machinery thus set in motion is so finely tuned that the script's rather operetta-ish plot is tinged with a curious asperity from the brutal economy of the *mise-en-scène*. For instance in the scene where, avoiding his wife's eye after being caught in the act of an adulterous misdemeanour, the pastor hides behind a huge tapestry at which an old servant is working who discomfits him by suddenly seizing his hand and revealing her shaming presence.

This gravity with which the comedy is thus weighted should doubtless be taken as a demonstration of the profoundly Protestant character of Dreyer's *oeuvre*, confirmed rather than invalidated by the many subversions that challenge it. An *oeuvre*, preeminently, of mortified flesh, condemned to the chastisements of shame and suffering (*Gertrud, Day of Wrath*), unless joyously consummated in the blessed fecundity of marriage (the Inger-Mikkel couple in *Ordet*).

A film which finally confirms the genius of Dreyer's sense of the plastic and, more particularly, defines one of the poles of his register. Whereas *Jeanne d'Arc* offers a pure plastic effect *independent of any light*, and *Vampyr* a play of white and black independent of any naturalism in the lighting, here we have a third form of exemplary experimentation: a *natural* play of lighting or, at least, one where any abstraction tends towards the natural. The exteriors (no matter whether the sun is real or otherwise) luminous to the point of dazzlement, the house crepuscular to the point of mystery. Never has Dreyer seemed so Dutch.'

Two of Dreyer's early films present women in apparently powerful roles, humiliating a central male protagonist into some accomodation to their needs/desires. *Master of the House* presents a patriarchal figure so tyrannical that the life of his wife, the survival of the family is endangered. *The Parson's Widow* presents an apparently matriarchal figure, Dame Margaret, whom one must marry if one is to become Pastor and who has already outlived several such candidates. She manages to confound her husband's adulterous schemes, but nevertheless when his passion has been socialised, she dies and he is finally able to marry his girl-friend. Margaret is a victim of that primitive patriarchal law (commented on in *All that Heaven Allows:* 'that old Egyptian custom of burying a husband's wife together with his possessions'—I quote from memory) which locates woman as part of the husband's property. In this case, the church is the representative of patriarchy.

The husband, Sofren's desire is a—social. He comes from Nature, as suggested by the mountains and waterfalls of the opening shots, with ragged clothes and no food or money, accompanied by his girl-friend. He accepts marriage because he's starving and drunk. The film links the socialisation of his desire to the institution of marriage, where, among other things, one realises there are 'higher' things than sexuality.

*   *   *

1921 Die Gezeichneten

(Love One Another)

Production	Primusfilm (Berlin)
Producer	Otto Schmidt
Script	Dreyer. Based on the novel by Aage Madelung
Director of Photography	Friedrich Weinmann
Art Director	Jens G. Lind

Polina Piekowska (*Hanna-Liebe*), Vladimir Gajdarov (*Jakov Segal*), Torleif Reiss (*Aleksander 'Sascha' Sokolov*), Richard Boleslawski (*Fedja*), Duwan (*The Merchant Suckoswerski*), Johannes Meyer (*Klimov, alias Rylovitch, alias Father Roman*), Adele Reuter-Eichberg (*Hanna's mother*), Emmy Wyde, Friedrich Kühne, Hugo Döblin. Running time: 105 mins.

As Dreyer pointed out, the film was made with a number of refugee artists from the 1917 Revolution: 'Bolevslavski and Gadarov, the two principal actors, as well as Polina Piekovska, were Russian. Duvan was also known. He had been the director of the Russian cabaret *The Bluebird*. As for the others, they were Russian, Danish, German and Norwegian. Besides that, the film was made in Berlin. But the film was adapted from an enormous novel (*Die Gezeichneten*, which sort of means *The Stigmatized Ones*), which we had to compress a great deal. Perhaps it was wrong to want to condense this big work in order to make a film out of it. It was necessary to cut, to prune, endlessly . . . This proves that novels shouldn't be filmed. It's too hard. I prefer to film theatre'. In his article *Among Russian Emigré in Berlin*, published in *Cahiers du Cinéma*, nr 207, Dreyer made a point of expressing his political sympathies with the White Russian emigrés.

The story of the film can be summarised as follows: Hannah-Liebe is a jewish child living in the ghetto of a small Russian provincial town. Anti-Jewish feeling is such that she is unable to attend the Russians' school. It also bars friendships with Russian children, including one peasant boy, Fedja, who fancies her. Hannah falls in love with Sascha, but because of gossip about their interracial friendship, he leaves for St. Petersburg. She follows later, to avoid an arranged marriage, visiting her brother Segal who has accepted Christianity for social and business purposes. Segal finds lodging for her in the home of a scientist, Lorov, and his wife. There she meets Sascha again. He has become a member of a revolutionary club, and they both join in its activities. Fedja, disguised as a monk, informs the authorities about Sascha's ideas and he is arrested together with Sascha. Segal succeeds in freeing his sister, but as Jews they are both deported to their home town, where they find their mother dying. Fedja also returns to the village, trying to incite the peasants against the Jewish community. A pogrom begins in which many Jews, including Segal, are shot. Hannah-Liebe falls into Fedja's hands but is rescued from that fate worse than death by Sascha, who has been liberated in a general strike which marks the beginning of the revolution of 1905.

What troubles this text appears to be the assertion of feminine desire across class and racial boundaries. Hannah falls in love with Sascha, a bourgeois Russian, and rejects the peasant-boy, Fedja. This opposition is made quite clear via an alternating syntagm, cutting from the couple Sascha-Hannah, walking by the water (signifier of desire, as always when we come across images of water in Dreyer's films) to a peasant girl attracted to Fedja who is lying, stretched out on the grass, both sensually less restrained than the quasi-bourgeois couple. Hannah's relation with Sascha is acceptable within revolutionary circles, but it also provides the possibility of revenge by Fedja. The pogrom he initiates involves murder of the Jews and rape of Hannah. His posing as a monk recalls Ivan in *Leaves from Satan's Book* but this time he is on the anti-revolutionary side.

In many ways this film resumes the concerns of *Leaves from Satan's Book*. Male desire is frustrated but finds an institutional pretext to achieve its aim, clearly designated as evil because of its sexuality and the crossing of class and racial barriers. We might note that racialism is absent from *Leaves from Satan's Book* while *Love One Another* could be regarded as the equivalent to the St Bartholomews episode in *Intolerance*.

The revolution, allowing for a last minute rescue, is clearly a *deus-ex-machina* to bring about the necessary tolerance invoked in the novel's title, *Love One Another*. But it is also the rescue of a woman by a man. The interests of patriachy, class (it is still a bourgeois revolution in many respects) and race are preserved in that order.

If Hannah is brought back within patriachal (though not Jewish) law, Segal, who has broken Jewish law by marrying a Christian wife and living like a Christian atones for this 'crime' by his own death in the pogrom. In this way, the fiction re-inscribes in its motivational logic the very theme the film is supposed to condemn. Indeed, if it is 'evil' to uphold the Jew/Gentile distinction (Fedja), why should Segal be punished for transgressing it?

*   *   *

1922 Der Var Engang

(Once Upon A Time)

Production	Sophus Madsen (Copenhagen)
Script	Dreyer, Palle Rosenkrantz. Based on the play by Holger Drachmann
Director of Photography	George Schnéevoigt
Art Director	Jens G. Lind
Editors	Dreyer, Edla Hansen

Clara Pontoppidan (*The Princess of Illyria*), Svend Methling (*The Prince of Denmark*), Peter Jerndorff (*The King*), Hakon Ahnfelt-Rønne (*Kaspar Roghat*), Karen Poulsen, Gerda Madsen.

This film was based on a play of the same title by Holger Drachmann (1846–1908). E. L. Bresdorff, in the *Penguin Guide to European Literature*, characterised Drachmann as 'by turns a socialist, a radical and realist disciple of George Brandes, a traditionalist praising marriage and home, a neo-romantic fairy-tale playwright, a bohemian poet inspired by a music hall singer'. The theme of the play, as it can be deduced from the surviving fragments of the film, does not come from Drachmann's socialist period, concerning as it does the 'taming of a shrew': a princess forced into domesticity by a prince who abducts her, and who learns to love her oppression and oppressor.

It is difficult to assess Ebbe Neergaard's claim that the lyrical quality of Drachmann's dialogue could not be transposed into silent-film. Certainly in the register of photography, George Schnéevoigt's photography is very lyrical indeed. The opening court scene shows Dreyer ably directing farcical comedy.

* * *

1924 Michael

Production	Decla-Bioscop for UFA (Berlin)
Producer	Erich Pommer
Script	Dreyer, Thea von Harbou. Based on the novel by Herman Bang.
Directors of Photography	Karl Freund (interiors), Rudolph Maté (some exteriors)
Art Director	Hugo Häring
Music	Hans Joseph Vieth

Benjamin Christensen (*Claude Zoret*), Walter Slezak (*Michael*), Nora Gregor (*The Princess Zamikow*), Robert Garrison (*Switt*), Grete Mosheim (*Alice Adelsskjold*), Didier Aslan (*Duc de Monthieu*), Karl Freund (*Leblanc, the art dealer*), Mady Christians.

Running time: 1966 m.

The main essay in this booklet discusses this film at some length. However, Dreyer's remarks, especially his comments on the use of decor, are worth quoting at some length: 'For *Michael*, I had a practically free hand. As for their success, the first was well enough received by the public but it was, above all, *Michael* that was a big critical success in Germany. It was called the first *Kammerspiel* (chamber music?) film, and I was very flattered by that, for this film was very important to me. The action takes place during a period when passion and exaggeration were in fashion, when feelings were willfully exacerbated; a period with a certain very false manner, which is seen in its decoration with all its outrageously supercharged interiors. The author of the novel, Herman Bang, belonged to the same period as Hjalmar Söderberg, the author of *Gertrud*, and it was even said of Söderberg that he imitated Bang, although it was Bang who imitated Söderberg. Well, it turns out that they knew each other and were even very friendly.

It was, for example, the period when, in France, the monasteries were expropriated by the government. Piles of accessories that came from churches and monasteries were put up for sale, and many people bought sacerdotal ornaments, chairs, benches and other furniture. For example, I knew a Danish actress who, when she moved back to Copenhagen, set herself up in an apartment filled with horrible things of this genre, all lighted by a bunch of chandeliers. Well, all that was also part of the film's atmosphere which reflects this rich taste . . . which was in bad taste but which, obviously was considered excellent at that time.

I collaborated on the decors but they were done by an architect who understood my intentions very well and who was absolutely amazing. This was Hugo Häring. He had never done decor for the cinema, and after that he never did any again, for following *Michael*, he went back to his true métier, to being an architect. For him, it was an *entracte* in his career (and the period was not so much one for the construction of new houses), an amusement, a fantasy that offered itself . . .

As principal actor in the role of Zoret, I took a Danish film director: Benjamin Christensen, the director of *Witchcraft Through the Ages*. In the role of Michael, there was young Walter Slezak, whom you must know for his American films. It was also the debut for cameraman Rudolf Maté. Before that, he had done only one short. In fact, Maté did not work on the whole film. Karl Freund was the cameraman who actually was supposed to do the film but he was obliged to leave, as he had other work to do. That is when it was proposed that Maté do the last takes. I was very satisfied with him and took him for my following film, *Joan of Arc*.'

*　　*　　*

1925 Du Skal Aere Din Hustru

(Master of the House/Thou Shalt Honour Thy Wife)

Production	Palladium Film (Copenhagen)
Script	Dreyer, Svend Rindom. Based on the play *Tyrännens Fald* by Svend Rindom.
Director of Photography	George Schnéevoigt
Art Director	Dreyer

Johannes Meyer (*Victor Frandsen*), Astrid Holm (*Ida*), Karin Nellemose (*Karen*), Mathilde Nielsen (*Mads, the nanny*), Aage Hoffman and Byril Harvig (*The Boys*), Clara Schønfeld (*Ida's mother*), Petrine Sonne (*The Washerwoman*), Johannes Nielsen (*The Doctor*).

Running time: 107 mins.

This film's use of comedy in a working class milieu and its combination of realism with naturalism were particularly successfully received in France, where Renoir's first films were just beginning to be shown. Its success prompted *Société Générale des*

Films to invite Dreyer to France to make his first large budget film, *The Passion of Joan of Arc*.

Master of the House could still be of use within the women's movement today, because, operating within an extremely humorous fictional form, it breaks down a woman's role into its component elements, clearly showing up the cash value of each element. Incidentally, it is worth noting that in some versions, the names of the characters have been anglicised: Ida becomes Mary, Victor becomes John, Karen changes to Kathleen, Mads changes to Nana Marsh, etc. Similarly, the anglicised version's undertitles are not always translations from the original Danish ones.

The title which opens the English version sets the tone of the film: 'This is the story of a spoilt husband, a type that is extinct in this country, but still exists abroad . . . And it is the story also of a heroine . . . not the brilliant, beautifully groomed and shingled heroine of the film play—but just an ordinary wife and mother whose life is compassed by the four walls of her suburban home' . . . 'Because Mary faced the sacrifices, the heavy tasks, the drab monotony so cheerfully, John, her husband, had come to take everything for granted'

In an interview in *Cahiers du Cinéma*, Dreyer referred to the film as a good example of his drive towards purification: 'In a theatre play, there are always so many little inessential things. Well, everything that is not absolutely necessary is a stumbling block. Things that block the way must be removed. The path must be clear, and lead towards what is essential, which is at the end of the road. When you take a theatrical dialogue there are too many accessory possibilities in it. And there is too much risk, in an adaptation, that the words, the sentences will be lost. It calls for pruning in such a way that what remains has an importance. By purification I want to make it possible for the spectator, who is following the images, the words and the intrigue, to have an open path so that he may get to the end of the road. It is for him that the dialogue must, so to speak, be put in close-ups.

In the theatre, you have time to write, time to linger on words and feelings, and the spectator has time to perceive these things. In the cinema it is different. This is why I have always concentrated on the purification of the text, which I compress to the minimum. I did this as early as *Master of the House*, for example, which was also originally a play. We compressed it, cleaned it, purified it and the story became very clear, very clean. That was the first time I employed this method. Later, I employed it for *Day of Wrath*, *Ordet*, *Gertrud*, which are also plays.'

In the same magazine, Sylvie Pierre noted:

'Adapting a play for the silent cinema was a commonplace transaction (the theatre conceived as a reservoir for plots). And the film makers who fearlessly did so, whether *Hamlet* or *Macbeth*, seemed to take no note of the hazard involved in their dizzy leap from word to image. Dreyer is far removed from this "primitive" innocence, and all his work is acutely aware of the problems involved in this transition, haunted by the cinematic gain immanent in their solution. Unless used as an entirely separate filmic space (as significant typography, *e.g.* Vertov, or as play on words, *e.g.* *Tire au flanc*), the inter-title is an emergency solution offering information at right angles to the image space. An expedient inevitable in certain cases, but a dangerous additive: easy for the film maker, wearying for the spectator. Using titles sparingly in *Master of the House*, Dreyer attempted to resolve the problem of the dialogue *within the shot*. His technique for doing so introduces an entirely original innovation to the expressionist method, which was to exaggerate dramatically all the silent signs negotiable as speech. Dreyer, without *provoking theatricality*, is content to define rather than stress these signs, to a point where they alone speak and the actors' lips parting in silence do not hinder the dialogue of expressions and gestures from functioning with serene clarity. For instance in the short and superb dialogue scene—but the dialogue is entirely *divined*—where the mother makes her son recite some lesson or other, lets him go, has second thoughts and calls him back for a last question, some snare, then finally packs him off, satisfied that he hasn't fallen into it.

Between words and gestures, things. The only consideration in the film, really, is shoes to be resoled, washing to hang up, butter to spread on slices of bread. And all this materiality, often making its own statement, supports and crystallises the drama.

A drama that is refined, of course, drained of any extraneous episodes, so that the "rudimentary" *semantic system can function as an energetic force rather than as a ponderous weight.'

*   *   *

1925 Glomdalsbruden

(The Bride of Glomdal)

Production	Victoria-Film (Oslo)
Script	Dreyer. Based on the stories, *Glomdalsbruden* and *Eline Vangel* by Jacob Breda Bull
Director of Photography	Einar Olsen
Art Director	Dreyer

Stub Wiberg (*Ole Glomgaarden*), Tove Tellback (*Berit, his daughter*), Harald Stormoen (*Jacob Braaten*), Einar Sissener (*Tore, his son*), Einar Tveito (*Gjermund Haugsett*), Rasmus Rasmussen (*The Pastor*), Sofi Reimers (*The Pastor's Wife*), Alfhild Stormoen (*Kari, Braaten's Wife*), Oscar Larsen (*Berger Haugsett*).
Length: 1237 m.

This film is much more than the 'little intermezzo' it is sometimes made out to be. Shot in one Norwegian summer, it is regarded as the film where Dreyer comes closest to Stiller, its sensuality and spontaneity surpassing Stiller in Dreyer's 'attention to texture and density of emotion' as Tom Milne puts it. In fact critics have speculated that the comparative absence of repression, the film's celebration of 'innocent' adolescent sexuality, might be connected with Dreyer's improvisational film making procedures.

The story concerns the love of Torre, a poor farmer's son, for Berit, the daughter of a neighbouring rich farmer. The families are symbolically separated by a river which, as usual in Dreyer, is a setting for the *mise-en-scène* of desire, including a final bravura struggle against its current.

The disruption which this narrative is designed to evacuate or contain is provided by the central couple's insufficiently socialised desire in the face of an excessively repressive patriachy. The fathers of Berit and another local boy, Gjermund, had already agreed on a deal involving the marriage of their children. In fact, the representatives of patriachy overstepped the bounds by omitting to consult Berit, an

---

*For the use of this term in connection with Dreyer, see André Téchiné's article reprinted as an appendix in this booklet.

51

'oversight' for which they can be prosecuted, according to the pastor. When Berit refuses to be handed over as a piece of property, she is disowned by her father and looked after by Torre's family. When Torre and Berit's love threatens to exceed the bounds of this arrangement, she is taken in by the pastor's family where the appropriate degree of moral authority can be applied to channel the erotic relationship into a socially sanctioned format.

The film clearly equates sociality with a degree of balance between the paternal and the maternal, in the sense that 'rampant' patriarchy is condemned in the tyrannical fathers and replaced by the feminised pastor's family. In other words, the correct type of patriarchal law must allow for a degree of heterogeneity by accommodating a necessary feminine element. The point is reemphasised when Torre and Berit enter into sociality via their marriage performed by the pastor, a ritual from which the parents are excluded.

Another interesting aspect of the film is its unstable system of eyeline matches and point-of-view structures. It would appear that in general, the matching adheres more rigorously to the rules of classic fictional cinema when the dramatisation of space requires it, *i.e.* when the two sides, Torre's and Berit's families, are opposed to each other. It is perhaps ironic that a disjunction in the diegesis is emphasised by means of a strict adherence to rules of editing designed to bind together, to unify. This underlines the point that the system of eyeline matches used in classic cinema, usually described as a procedure to hermetically seal, close off the diegesis, in fact constitutes a procedure to bind *the spectator* into the fiction. In other words, classic editing systems do not necessarily unify contradictions within the *énoncé* (the diegesis), but they appear to function primarily as means of papering over the potentially disruptive split between *énoncé* and *énonciation* (between what is narrated and the process of narration).

*   *   *

1927 La Passion de Jeanne d'Arc

(The Passion of Joan of Arc)

Production	Société Générale des Films (Paris)
Script	Dreyer, Joseph Delteil. Based on the original records of the trial (and supposedly on two novels, *Vie de Jeanne d'Arc* and *La Passion de Jeanne d'Arc* by Joseph Delteil).
Director of Photography	Rudolph Maté
Art Directors	Hermann Warm, Jean Hugo
Music	Victor Alix, Léo Pouget

Maria Falconetti (*Joan of Arc*), Eugène Silvain (*Pierre Cauchon*), Maurice Schutz (*Nicholas Loyseleur*), Michel Simon (*Jean Lemaître*), Antonin Artaud (*Massieu*), Ravet (*Jean Beaupère*), André Berley (*Jean d'Estivet*), Jean d'Yd (*Guillaume Evrard*), André Lurville, Jacques Arna, Alexandre Mihalesco, R. Narlay, Henri Maillard, Jean Aymé, Léon Larive, Henri Gaultier and Paul Jorge (*Judges*).

Asked about the production circumstances of the film, Dreyer explained:

'When I arrived in France, in order to make a film for the *Société Générale des Films*, I proposed three subjects. One on Marie Antoinette, another on

Catherine de Medici, and the third on Joan of Arc. I had several interviews with the people at the *Société Générale* but we couldn't arrive at a choice of subject. Then someone said, "Let's take three matches, and draw." I agreed. We drew. I got the headless match: it was *Joan of Arc. Joan of Arc* was a big thing for me. Previous to that I had never undertaken such a big film. I had a free hand, I did absolutely what I wanted and, at that time, I was very satisfied with what I had done.

For me, it was, before all else, the technique of the official report that governed. There was, to start with, this trial, with its ways, its own technique, and that technique is what I tried to transpose to the film. There were the questions, there were the answers—very short, very crisp. There was, therefore no other solution than to place close-ups behind these replies. Each question, each answer, quite naturally called for a close-up. It was the only possibility. All of that stemmed from the technique of the official report. In addition, the result of the close-ups was that the spectator was shocked as Joan was, receiving the questions, tortured by them. And, in fact, it was my intention to get this result.

Cahiers: The thing that the heroines of Day of Wrath *and* Joan of Arc *had in common is that they were both accused of sorcery . . .*

Dreyer: Yes. And both ended on the stake . . . Except that Lisbeth Movin didn't come to it in the same fashion . . . Moreover, I envisaged another ending for *Day of Wrath* that I found nicer. You didn't see the sorceress going to the stake. You only heard a young choir boy singing the Dies Irae and, from this, you understood that she, too, was destined for the flames. However, the actual ending, in certain respects, appeared to me to be necessary. It was necessary to give a material form to the consequences of this intolerance.

With Falconetti, it often happened that, after having worked all afternoon, we hadn't succeeded in getting exactly what was required. We said to ourselves then: tomorrow we will begin again. And the next day, we would have the bad take from the day before projected, we would examine it, we would search and we always ended by finding, in that bad take, some little fragments, some little light that rendered the exact expression, the tonality we had been looking for. It is from there that we would set out again, taking the best and abandoning the remainder. . .

Cahiers: How did you discover that Falconetti had something to give?

Dreyer: I went to see her one afternoon and we spoke together for an hour or two. I had seen her at the theatre. A little boulevard theatre whose name I have forgotten. She was playing there in a light, modern comedy and she was very elegant in it, a bit giddy, but charming. She didn't conquer me at once and I didn't have confidence in her immediately. I simply asked her if I could come to see her the next day. And, during that visit, we talked. That is when I sensed that there was something in her to which one could make an appeal. Something that she could give: something, therefore, that I could take.

For, behind the make-up, the pose, behind that modern and ravishing appearance, there was something. There was a soul behind that façade. If I could see her remove the façade it would suffice me. So I told her that I would very much like, starting the next day, to do a screen test with her. "But without make-up," I added, "with your face completely naked."

She came, therefore, the next day ready and willing. She had taken off her make-up, we made the tests, and I found on her face exactly what I had been seeking for Joan of Arc: a rustic woman, very sincere, who was also a woman

53

who had suffered. But even so, this discovery did not represent a total surprise to me for, from our first meeting, this woman was very frank and, always, very surprising.

I therefore took her for the film, we always understood each other very well, we constantly worked very well. It has been said that it was I who squeezed the lemon.

I have never squeezed the lemon. I never squeezed anything. She always gave freely, with all her heart. For her heart was always committed to what she was doing.'

The Passion of Joan of Arc is Dreyer's perhaps most discussed and most regularly screened film, a 'monument' of film history, a monumentality from which I find it difficult to disengage. It is a film which awaits another history of the cinema, some reassessment of the history of avant-garde and independent cinema. One thing is certain, this is not an independently produced film, but a 'mainstream' industrial product, regarded by Dreyer as his commercial breakthrough, and critics wishing to categorise the film as avant-garde, experimental etc. must take this crucial economic and ideological fact into consideration.

As Paul Willemen suggested to me during the production of this booklet:

'What appears to have disoriented journalists and critics, provoking the labels "art" and "experiment" (journalistic dumping grounds for all films not adhering totally to rules codified in Hollywood) is Dreyer's tentative emphasis within a commercial fiction film, on the poetic function of discursive practice. In other words, the process of enunciation is foregrounded and at times aggressively impinges upon the narrative, reversing the usual relation of dominance between the two levels.

The trial, Joan's passion, which constitutes that narrative, results in her apparent submission. She accepts the removal of her man's clothing—a sign of the "trouble" she causes—and makes the transition to the "appropriate" place of women, *i.e.* that of suffering femininity. The degree of suffering involved in that submission forcing her retraction and her final annihilation. In fact the image of the burning is particularly significant in the Dreyer-text. Joan is punished for her daring to demand and assume the supreme signifier of desire, the phallus (in her man's clothing). By "unmasking" her, the male inquisition defines her as a woman, but she still remains a desiring woman. This means that when she arrives at the place the male order reserves for the female (*i.e.* a place defined by patriarchy as "elsewhere" as outside) her passion, her desire can only be eradicated, effaced by the disintegration of her very body. A purification by fire in which the fire functions as a double edged image.

As the male/symbolic order is there to contain desire, the female, identified with the danger of the breakthrough of pure desire/the semiotic, when "put in her place" by patriarchy, cannot but be engulfed by the "fires" of desire. In this way, the fire is in fact a male signifier for representing female desire. It is in this trouble of the feminine, the motor of the fiction, which also constitutes the "trouble" of the narration, disrupting the "impersonal", god-like narration characteristic of classic cinema, and thus foregrounding the process of enunciation, the discursive process itself. But once again the discursive marks double the "trouble" of the fiction: the sadistic aggression on the body of the fictional Joan perpetrated by the inquisitors, is doubled by the cinematic aggression of the image of Joan/Falconetti, aggressing the integrity of her face. Other examples are provided by the fragmentation of the image where a "classic" style would have striven towards homogeneity, as pointed out by Tom Milne in his book on Dreyer when he refers to "the irritating cross cutting which ruins the beautiful scene where Joan smiles at seeing a cross on the floor of her cell made by the shadow of her barred window, fragmenting it *unnecessarily!*" (my emphasis). This scene in fact offers a double fragmentation: the syntagmatic fragmentation produced by the cross-cutting and the compositional fragmentation of the image.'

*　　*　　*

1932 Vampyr

Production	Tobis-Klangfilm (Berlin) and Carl Dreyer Filmproduktion (Paris).
Producers	Dreyer, Nicolas de Gunzburg
Script	Dreyer, Christen Jul. Freely adapted from the collection of short stories by Sheridan Le Fanu, *Through a Glass Darkly*
Directors of Photography	Rudolph Maté, Louis Neé
Art Directors	Hermann Warm, Hans Bittmann, Cesare Silvagni
Music	Wolfgang Zeller

Julian West, *i.e.* Nicolas de Gunzburg (*David Gray*), Henriette Gérard (*Marguerite Chopin, the Vampire*), Jan Hieronimko (*The Doctor*), Maurice Schutz (*The owner of the castle*), Sybille Schmitz (*Léonce*), Rena Mandel (*Gisèle*), Albert Bras and A. Babanini (*Servants*), Jane Mora (*The nurse*).
Running time: 70 mins.

My detailed analysis of *Vampyr* (*Screen*, vol. 17 nr. 3) discussing its point-of-view structures and its discursive system, concluded with the following remarks:

Todorov divides the content of the literary fantastic into two semantic classes, themes of the 'I' and themes of the 'you', the 'non-I'. The former class are concerned with the structuring of the relationship between man and the world, the world perceived through his eyes, his 'I', his consciousness, the relation of the structuring subject to its objects. The fantastic tends to put this relationship into question, the problem of vision becoming a main thematic. The latter class concern the dynamic relations of human action in the world through the mediation of others, and are characterised in the fantastic by themes of discourse and desire, the latter in excessive forms as well as in its various transformations (perversions) in themes of cruelty, violence, death, life after death, corpses and vampires. On the expression plane, these are arranged by the use of the narrative sub-code, often as first-person narration. As far as the text of *Vampyr* is concerned, the themes of the cinematic fantastic are similar to those of the literary fantastic. The pronoun functions, part of the narrative sub-code, which also includes the *grande syntagmatique* insofar as it is applicable, are necessary for narration, though not specific to the fantastic. The interventions of *discours* create disruptions in the plane of expression corresponding to those on the plane of content, and as such the interventions of *discours* participate in the realisation of the fantastic in this particular text. In addition, however, these marks of

55

authorial presence function as part of an authorial code/sub-code which can be shown to have other manifestations in this and other texts, thematically—*e.g.* 'narcissism', a concern common to the fantastic and to other texts by Dreyer—and structurally—*e.g.* the 'disruptive' continuities in *Joan of Arc*.

It might seem appropriate to separate more clearly two 'levels' of uncertainty in the text: that relating to the status of what Gray sees (is the father 'real', is the body in the coffin 'real'?); and that relating to the 'undermining' of the position of the reader, who is in a relation of uncertainty to the whole text as is Gray to his part in it, the reader not knowing how to read the whole text which includes the uncertainty of David Gray about his own perceptions. Analysis of other cinefantastic texts would enable one to establish whether the configuration of character 'I' and authorial 'I' peculiar to *Vampyr* is also characteristic of the genre. One could certainly imagine a text using only 'conventional' coding still raising issues of uncertainty by refusing to mark sections as to whether they pertain to dream or to reality. One could also imagine the reverse, for instance E. T. A. Hoffman's *The Sandman* rewritten by James Joyce so that the problematic of vision would effect systematic displacements at the level of spelling, choice of substantives referring to vision, syntax, and so on, yet the structure as a fantastic text would remain the same. Whether the insistence of *discours* is specific to the economy of *Vampyr* as a metonymic displacement from the uncertainty at the level of content, or is rather characteristic of the cinefantastic as a genre, can only be deduced after analysis of other possible members of that genre, which has yet to be done. At the present stage the demands of economy in analysis require the hypothesis of a code of pronoun functions to cover both these types of facts.

The fantastic is predicated on the category of reality: 'The reader and the hero ... must decide if a certain event or phenomenon belongs to reality or to imagination, that is, must determine whether or not it is real. It is therefore the category of the real which has furnished a basis for our definition of the fantastic' (Todorov).* A dialectic between the categories of the real and the unreal characterised the thinking of the 19th century: '. . . In a metaphysics of the real and the imaginary, and the literature of the fantastic is nothing but the bad conscience of this positivist era' (Todorov). The 20th century, on the contrary, has tended to emphasise the autonomy of the text from any 'real' referent; it is the era of the modernist text, of Joyce, the *nouveau roman*, etc. In the cinema, however, this 19th century debate persists in the issue of realism, the problem of the 'reality' of the cinematic referent. The fantastic text is not modernist in the sense say of Robbe-Grillet's *L'Immortelle,* where there is only a reversible series of representations, where the issue of diegetic reality is irrelevant, but it is progressive in that in it the category of the real is at least under scrutiny.

Now, having further investigated the structures of subjectivity at play in the Dreyer-text, the above conclusion appears, although still valid, to be stopping short at a somewhat formalist level of analysis.

Vampyr does indeed function according to the rules which Tzvetan Todorov found to be characteristic of the fantastic in literature, *i.e.* the systematic inscription of hesitation. The question of the reality status of the fictional events is constantly posed to the implied reader, who is then forced to hesitate between mutually

*The book referred to is: Tzvetan Todorov, *The fantastic, a Structural Approach to a Literary Genre*, Cleveland, Ohio, 1975.

exclusive explanations: in this event 'real' or 'supernatural'? This type of systematic undercutting of certainty occurs in a number of Dreyer's films, *e.g. Joan of Arc, Ordet, Day of Wrath, They Caught the Ferry*. It also occurs in *Gertrud* in the form of the question: What is real for the subject? or rather, what is real for Gertrud? who, in the words she is forced to misrecognise as hers, has never lived. The most striking inscriptions of this principle of hesitation in Dreyer's films, opening up an understanding of what is at stake beyond a mere formalist identification of the strategy, resolves around problems of witchcraft. The previous notes on the Dreyer-text showed that witchcraft functions as a terrain on which social definitions of sexed identity intersect with the fundamental bisexuality of desire as libidinal energy. It is perhaps another merit of the Dreyer-text that it so clearly draws attention to the questions underlying Todorov's principle of uncertainty: the questions provoked by the fantastic as a genre are not simply of the order: is this real, or not?, but directly address the question of the sexed identity of the subject. The process of the socialisation of desire, its containment by and within the cultural order, clearly implies a fixing of what is male and/or female. Transgressions of this rigorously enforced cultural distinction between sex-roles are punished in several ways (e.g. *Joan of Arc*, the witches in *Day of Wrath* and *Vampyr*, who all exceed the limitations imposed on female desire by the male order). In fact, the questions provoked in the implied viewer by the structure of the fantastic text, are diegeticised in Dreyer's films in the form of a confusion of sex-roles or identities: Joan of Arc is dressed in man's clothing, the 'Vampyr' is of an indeterminate sex. In return, this direct diegetic representation of the question: what sex is this person?, rebounds on the viewer, who is at the other end of the look binding text and spectator together, and is there transformed into the question: what sex am I? Or, in simpler terms, it raises the problem of bisexuality and its mode of representation, of inscription in discursive systems.

*   *   *

1942 Mødrehjaelpen

(Good Mothers)

Production	Mogens Skot-Hansen Nordisk Films Kompagni for Dansk Kulturfilm and Ministeriernes Filmudvalg.
Script	Dreyer
Director of Photography	Verner Jensen, Poul Gram
Music	Poul Schierbeck
Narrator	Ebbe Neergaard

Running time: 12 mins.

During the Nazi occupation, the state production of documentary films, insisting on a clear and socially conscious line, was intended as a discreet countermeasure to Nazi newsreels. *Good Mothers* is a good instance of this, describing, through the experiences of one mother, the social facilities of pre- and post-natal care available. The celebrated 'autonomy' of Dreyer's camera is much in evidence. As in a number of his short films, the role of music is important in giving the film a unity it might otherwise not possess. In this case, that unity is the all too familiar ideology of 'the state cares for everyone'. In a slightly modified form and with an English commentary, this film was also nr. 2 in the *Social Denmark* series of documentaries.

*   *   *

1943 Vredens Dag

(Day of Wrath)

Production	Palladium Film
Script	Dreyer, Mogens Skot-Hansen, Poul Knudsen. Based on the play *Anne Pedersdotter* by Hans Wiers-Jenssen.
Director of Photography	Karl Andersson
Art Director	Erik Aaes, Lis Fribert
Music	Poul Schierbeck
Editors	Edith Schlüssel, Anne Marie Petersen

Thorkild Roose (*Absalon Pedersson*), Lisbeth Movin (*Anne Pedersdotter*), Sigrid Neiiendam (*Merete, Absalon's mother*), Preben Lerdorff Rye (*Martin*), Anna Svierkier (*Marte Herlof*), Albert Høberg (*The Bishop*), Olaf Ussing (*Laurentius*), Sigurd Berg (*Choirmaster*).
Running time: 100 mins.

In an interview with *Cahiers du Cinéma*, Dreyer made the following points about the aesthetics of composition and rhythm:

D. '. . . in a long shot the rhythm comes automatically with movement.'

CdC. '*In the horizontal travelling shots, you say that the eye easily follows objects . . . but there are moments when the eye is stopped by verticals.*'

D. 'That's how one obtains a dramatic effect. In *Day of Wrath* the witch is tied onto a long ladder, which is vertical and stays there just until the signal to let her fall is given, and then this change gives a great dramatic effect,—that's the vertical effect.'

CdC. '*You play with vertical and horizontal lines. In doing so, do you know exactly what effect you are going to obtain?*'

D. 'Yes, I think so. In *Day of Wrath*, I started to use long shots with slowish rhythm, because when serious things are in question, the replies mustn't come too quick: in this type of film one must have time to hear and understand the reply, not let the word on the screen escape.'

In '*A Little on Film Style*' (1943), Dreyer develops these points at some length, elaborating on the formal values of horizontal and vertical, the rhythm and length of shot. Regarding oppositions between *Day of Wrath* and his traditional procedure of purification, he commented:'

'*Day of Wrath* was a play I saw in 1920. But, at that time, it was still too soon to make the film. Therefore I put the play in a drawer and, later, in 1943–1944, I took it up again and began thinking about how one might transpose it, as cinematically as possible. For that, I was obliged to proceed exactly as I had already done previously, but even more so: I had to clean the text as much as possible.

If I proceed in this way, it is because I believe that in the cinema, one may not permit what is permissible in the theatre. In the theatre, you have words. And the words fill the space, hang in the air. You can hear them, feel them, experience their weight. But in the cinema the words are very quickly relegated to a background which absorbs them and that is why you may retain only words which are absolutely necessary. The essential is sufficient.'

Jean-Louis Cornolli regarded *Day of Wrath* as the key to Dreyer's work. He wrote:

'A focal point in an *oeuvre* to which it is manifestly the key—a readily decipherable blueprint—*Day of Wrath* simultaneously assembles, organises and defines the signals coming (of course) from *Joan of Arc* and *Leaves from Satan's Book*, and in its turn irradiates *Ordet* and even *Gertrud*—in Anne, the heroine of *Day of Wrath*, there is something, though in a natural and almost savage state, of Gertrud. But the relationship to *Vampyr*, though less direct, proves to be even more fertile. In a sense *Day of Wrath* shows the diurnal, "sacred" or "sublime" side of the same conflict between the "innocent" and the "devotees" (of blood in one film, of Christ in the other, each akin to the other, indeed exact equivalents on the level of myth, and equivalent furthermore in their terrorism): a tragedy (classical in every sense) as opposed to *Vampyr*'s tale of the fantastic (in direct descent from the corresponding German literary genre); harsh, violent contrasts between black and white, as opposed to their equivocal marriage in the greys of *Vampyr*.

But superimposing these two films also brings out the exact contours of the theme of intolerance in *Day of Wrath* (and by extension in the entire *oeuvre*): it is both more and worse than the particular circumstance of a dogmatism run mad at a more or less specific historical time; it becomes the condition, even the rule of any society (whether that of the devout or that of the vampires), it is the terror which lies at the root of any order. "No intolerance, ideological intransigence or proselytism but reveals the brutish basis of enthusiasm," says Cioran. "One kills only in the name of a God or its imitations: the excesses aroused by the goddess Reason, by the idea of nation, class or race are akin to those of the Inquisition and the Reformation." The displacement is thus effected revealing that in Dreyer's work it is the face of authority in power (here priest and pastors, elsewhere politicians and bourgeois) that is aimed at and pierced behind the corporate mask of God.

What makes this displacement possible, curiously enough, is that *Day of Wrath* is one of the very rare films to answer the classical definitions of tragedy: from the outset, in fact, the conflict is established, the trap set, the outcome inevitable (and proclaimed by the mother); these are not "characters" confronting each other—so no psychological digression becomes necessary— but two antagonistic forces, two ideas: against the forces of life are ranged those of the repressive system; they are stated from the outset, integral, immutable, obdurate; but with the same inevitability that makes the initial malediction come true, the exception is defeated by the rule, and the logic of power destroys the revolt by life.

So the feeling of horror in *Day of Wrath*, the sense of intolerable tragedy, springs from nothing else but this ineluctable. It is not the witches who terrify but the arbiters of justice; and the "wrath of God" is only the more monstrous in being interpreted by these coldly frigid men (ghosts or vampires, already dead) as much as by these glacially chilling forms.'

The trials and burning of the witch are presented as the responsibility of men. Women may appear in the crowd, but that is all. Besides signifying 17th century patriarchal social relations with men representing both the law and God, this fact also dramatises, inversely, the mechanism of conversion hysteria. The woman who challenges the male order with her own desire, belief in her own power (Anne), insistence on masculine dress and her access to God unmediated by the (male) church (Joan), is represented to the social body as literally consumed in her (by definition) evil desire, so misrecognised by the social body that desire is 'thrown out' with the body of the woman, its constant return necessitating constant vigilance and the certainty of future victims.

The process of symptom formation in conversion hysteria is inscribed in the body of the text in the form of its obsessive return to the witch, emphasising that it isn't a matter of one individual witch, but a constant stream of women repressed in their own desire and marked by that of men. Indeed, witchcraft, the expression of desire, is considered to be contagious, as evidenced by the flame in Anne's eyes.

As desire begins to burn in Anne, *i.e.* as she claims the right to become a sexual being, the film's narrative and semantic structures once more betray the male cultural discourse presiding over its organisation. Although Anne's desire is positive in relation to the puritanical oppression incarnated by Absalon and the church fathers, but nevertheless rendered guilty because of the disturbing effects a 'sexual mother' is supposed to have on her son, Martin. His desire being provoked (in terms of the film) by Anne, he must leave the house. Indeed, it was this aspect of the film which was supposed to be of overwhelming interest to viewers in rural Italy, where it was released under the title: *The Lover of His Mother*.

*   *   *

1944 Två Människor

(Two People)

Production	Svensk Filmindustri (Stockholm)
Producer	Hugo Bolander
Script	Dreyer, Martin Glanner. Based on the play *Attentat* by W. O. Somín.
Director of Photography	Gunnar Fischer
Art Director	Nils Svenwall
Music	Lars-Erik Larsson
Editors	Dreyer, Edvin Hammarberg

Georg Rydeberg (*Dr. Arne Lidell*), Wanda Rothgardt (*Marianne*), Gabriel Alw. Running time: 78 mins.

Dreyer emphatically refuses any responsibility for this film: '[the film] doesn't exist:'

> *Cahiers du cinéma: 'But I've seen it. I am thus in the position of having a point of view. It exists.*
> *Dreyer:* You know, for this film, I was placed in a precarious situation. It was in 1944. I was told that perhaps I was in danger, because of the Germans. Therefore I left for Stockholm with *Day of Wrath*, for the official reason of selling the film. Then I stayed in Stockholm and wanted to make this little film. Unfortunately, the producer decided to choose the actors himself. He wanted a great career. Well, the actors in question represented the exact opposite of what I would have wanted. And, for me, the actors are extremely important. Thus, I wanted the woman to be a bit theatrical, a little hysterical, and, for the actor for the part of the scientist, I wanted a man with blue eyes, naïve but completely honest, who was interested in nothing but his work. Well, they gave me an actress who was the personification of a little bourgeoise and, for the man, instead of a blue-eyed idealist, I was given an intriguing demoniac with brown eyes . . .'

CdC: '*Don't you think that this film also has a certain relationship to Gertrud?*'
D: 'Oh no! There is absolutely no comparison. And it is a film that was doomed from the start, completely.'

The story is constructed around the events of a single day in the flat-*cum*-laboratory of a Swedish doctor, Arne Lidell, and which the camera never leaves except for a flashback, and in which his relationship with his wife, Marianne, is subjected to the pressure of a crime which threatens to overwhelm them both. The crime, the murder of a Professor Zander, who was apparently blackmailing Marianne threatening to reveal a past sexual relationship which ceased when she met Arne. His price was that she inform him of the results of Arne's work. She accepted his terms because she wanted their marriage to continue. So their marriage continues (if it was ever seriously threatened) at the price of Arne's work (cf *Gertrud* 'Women's love and men's work are enemies from the start'). The film sets up an equation between her childlessness and the destruction of his work (his symbolic child), a process most clearly marked in the final scene: the death of the couple shows her cradling Arne in her arms like a dead child, singing a lullaby to him as she dies. In other words, like Inger in *Ordet*, she becomes a mother as she dies.

This film appears the most melodramatic of all Dreyer's films. Its credit sequence contains images and music worthy of Douglas Sirk. Yet the articulation of the woman's point-of-view, so evident in Sirk's films, remains unclear—at least on one viewing. The film is also interesting for the rigour with which the tragic unities of space, time and place are maintained, disrupted only by the shadowy figure of Zander. The rest of the world only intrudes in the form of messages: letters, newspapers and the radio. Moreover, the camera-work and the way subjectivity is inscribed by/in relation to it, appears similar to the kind of disjunctions Burch and Dana described in *Gertrud*. *Two People* is not nearly as uninteresting as Dreyer makes out. It is only Dreyer who always insisted on total control, who would think of disclaiming responsibility for a film which he could only imperfectly control. If John Ford or Sternberg ever had been granted as much control over their work as Dreyer had over *Two People*...

*   *   *

1946 Vandet På Landet

(Water from the Land)

Production	Palladium Film for Ministeriernes Filmudvalg.
Script	Dreyer
Director of Photography	Preben Frank
Music	Poul Schierbeck
Narrators	Henrik Malberg, Asbjørn Andersen

Running time: 11 mins.

Water from the Land was begun under the occupation, but banned before release because of its disturbing/inaccurate picture of the health of the water supply in rural Denmark. The material in the Danish archive suggests that the film showed the contamination of a well by rats, human excreta and traffic, then the passage of that polluted water around the house and its connection with outbreaks of typhoid. One shot of a baby sucking a typhus infected sponge was probably too much for the authorities. It goes on to depict the building of a new system of water supply and the drilling of a new, more hygienic well. The source of the water supply and the percolation of surface water into the well are clearly illustrated with diagrams. The typhoid problem is highlighted by a montage of newspaper cuttings. It could have been a very useful and shocking film about the need for piped water and hygienic construction (and health education). Not particularly socially radical as a film on a similar topic by Joris Ivens would have been (no mention of the causes for people's ignorance, their lack of resources) the shots address the viewer via careful, slow panning movements.

*   *   *

1947 Landsbykirken

(The Danish Village Church)

Production	Preben Frank Film for Dansk Kulturfilm
Script	Dreyer, Bernhard Jensen.
Director of Photography	Preben Frank
Music	Svend Erik Tarp
Commentary	Dreyer, Ib Koch-Olsen
Narrator	Ib Koch-Olsen
Running Time: 14 mins.	

To a commentary by a parson, this film shows the development of rural church architecture from the earliest simple wooden churches to the present day. Using a model, this history is then reversed and a similar history of the changing interior, and relation of the audience to the ritual, from spectators to congregation, is presented. Throughout, the 'sparse' aesthetic of the Reformation receives a lot of emphasis. With its backward and forward movement, the film inscribes the continuity of the church's relation with the community and the libidinal investment it represents, creating a 'memory' of religion.

*   *   *

1947 Kampen mod Kraeften

(The Struggle Against Cancer)

Production	Preben Frank Film for Dansk Kulturfilm
Script	Dreyer, Carl Krebs
Director of Photography	Preben Frank
Music	Peter Deutsch
Narrator	Albert Luther
Running Time: 15 mins.	

*   *   *

1948 De Naede Faergen

(They Caught the Ferry)

Production	Dansk Kulturfilm for Ministeriernes Filmudvalg.
Script	Dreyer, based on a short story by Johannes V. Jensen.

Director of Photography Jørgen Roos
Running Time: 12 mins.

This film is basically an extension of a short story by J. V. Jensen, who received the Nobel prize for literature in 1944. It links the story of a motorcycling couple's encounter with death as they rush across an island to catch the ferry, to a moral lesson about speeding and road safety. There is virtually no dialogue, a fact which may account for much of the film's effectivity.

*   *   *

1949 Thorvaldsen

Production   Preben Frank Film for Dansk Kulturfilm
Script   Dreyer, Preben Frank
Director of Photography Preben Frank
Music   Svend Erik Tarp
Narrator   Ib Koch-Olsen
Running Time: 10 mins.

A documentary about the famous 19th century sculptor whose style was described in *The Oxford Companion to Art* as 'lucid and harmonious, perhaps over-studied' and 'somewhat anaemic by reason of the unrelieved whiteness.' This latter remark, juxtaposed to Dreyer's declaration of love for white walls, indicates why Dreyer may have been interested in Thorvaldsen's work. What the *Oxford Companion* described as 'over-studied' is in fact a particular combination of repression and sensual excess, another possible reason for Dreyer's interest. The film is about a few of Thorvaldsen's major pieces, including those executed for Copenhagen Cathedral. In its movement around the sculptures the camera creates an equivalence between itself and the imagined spectator's eyes caressing the sculpture.

*   *   *

1950 Storstrømsbroen

(The Storstrøm Bridge)
Production   Preben Frank Film for Dansk Kulturfilm
Script   Dreyer
Director of Photography Preben Frank
Music   Svend S. Schultz
Running Time: 7 mins.

This film continues the strategy of *Thorvaldsen*, *e.g.* the movement of the camera around an object (this time Denmark's longest bridge linking the islands of Seeland and Falster) which is fragmented by the montage of differently angled shots but 'reassembled' by the rhythm of camera movement and music. There is no commentary, as in Joris Ivens' *The Bridge*, but whereas that film betrayed a fascination with machinery and the functioning of the bridge as a means of communication in relation to road, rail and shipping traffic, *The Storstrøm Bridge* merely celebrates the existence of the bridge itself.

*   *   *

1957 Et Slot i et Slot

(The Castle within the Castle)

Production	Teknisk Film Co. for Dansk Kulturfilm
Script	Dreyer
Director of Photography	Jørgen Roos
Narrator	Sven Ludvigsen
Running Time: 9 mins.	

This is a useful 'architectural' film about the ruins of the castle 'Krogen' discovered within the Kronborg castle at Helsingør, which replaced it. Dreyer's mark can be seen in the carefulness of the lighting with characteristic pools of highlight, the simplicity of composition tending to the minimal, and the very slow camera pans. The use of dissolves and wipes to show architectural changes is very effective. As in *Danish Village Church* the film emphasises historical continuity.

*　　*　　*

1954 Ordet

(The Word)

Production	Palladium Film
Producer	Erik Nielsen
Script	Dreyer. Based on the play by Kaj Munk
Director of Photography	Henning Bendsten
Art Director	Erik Aaes
Music	Poul Schierbeck
Editor	Edith Schlüssel

Henrik Malberg (*Morten Borgen*), Emil Hass Christensen (*Mikkel*), Preben Lerdorff Rye (*Johannes*), Cay Kristiansen (*Anders*), Birgitte Federspiel (*Inger*), Ejner Federspiel (*Peter, the tailor*), Sylvia Eckhausen (*his wife Kirstine*), Gerda Nielsen (*Anne, his daughter*), Ove Rud (*The Pastor*), Henry Skjaer (*The Doctor*), Anne Elizabeth (*Maren*), Susanne (*little Inger*), Sylvia Eckhausen (*Peter's wife*), Hanne Aagesen (*Karen*), Edith Trane (*Mette Maren*).
Running time: 126 mins.

Regarding the history and the cultural impact of the religious conflict presented in *Ordet*, Dreyer said:

'I was so much happier doing *Ordet* when I felt myself very close to the conceptions of Kaj Munk. He always spoke well of love. I mean to say, of love in general, between people, as well as love in marriage, true marriage. For Kaj Munk, love was not only the beautiful and good thoughts that can link man and woman, but also a very profound bond. And for him there was no difference between sacred and profane love. Look at *Ordet*. The father is saying, "She is dead . . . she is no longer here. She is in heaven . . ." and the son answers, "Yes but I loved her body too . . ."

What is beautiful, in Kaj Munk, is that he understood that God did not separate these two forms of love. That is why he didn't separate them either. But this form of Christianity is opposed by another form, a somber and fanatic faith.'

Cahiers du cinéma: The first form relates, I believe, in Denmark, to the reform of Grundtvig, and the second to the ideas of the Interior Mission, born of the teachings of

Kierkegaard. These are the two forms that define—or defines—the Danish faith. Did you experience this opposition?'

D.: 'The latter form of Christianity, severe, often fanatic, which establishes a divorce between thought and action, is above all the faith of western Jutland. Me, I'm from Seeland . . . But I remember certain cases . . . Yes: one time in particular, an affair made quite a stir, born of the intransigence of a priest of the Interior Mission. He had given proof, in his church, of a particularly outrageous violence and harshness. The entire country was shocked by it. Everyone rose against this black Christianity. Everyone opposed him with the other form of Christianity: clear, joyous, illuminated . . . This is the antagonism incarnated by the rich farmer and the poor tailor.

But Kaj Munk, who obviously had sympathy for that bright form of Christianity (which, in the play, is that of the farmer), also had some for the other. He understood that there was much good faith among them, that they sincerely believed, acting as they did, they were living up to the mission of Jesus, which for them excluded indulgence. There was the same problem with this priest I spoke of, who was more Christian than Jesus himself; who burned, or believed he burned, with the same fire as he.'

CdC.: 'I believe that a large part of Danish literature at the end of the 19th century and the beginning of the 20th was influenced by this struggle.'

D.: 'Yes. Denmark was marked by a schism. In France you had something analogous at the time of Jansenism. For me, that also relates to a question I have always posed myself: that of tolerance and intolerance. That intolerance between two religious parties is a thing I did not like. Never have I accepted intolerance.

In *Day of Wrath*, for example, Christians show their intolerance for those who are attached to remnants of ancient religions, to superstitions.

In her review of the film, Sylvie Pierre attached less importance to the religious aspects of the film, focussing more on its construction and *mise-en-scène*:

'Its qualities too often evaluated on the same "elevated" level as its subject—and after all, expectations of tedium are surely justified concerning a film whose subject is no less than a miracle of faith—*Ordet* suffers, one might say, from too high a reputation. Happily, however, embalmed in respect, it is reborn again at each new viewing, as though the metaphor of its own life were being realised in its fiction.

As in all of Dreyer's films except *Vampyr*—even those where the script is not adapted, as here, from a play—the life in *Ordet* is first and foremost that of the theatre. For it has of course nothing to do with filmed theatre. If I examine the theatricality of *Ordet* (and not of *Gertrud*, even though more exemplary), it is because a number of affiliations, transpositions and metamorphoses make their appearance here in a particularly subtle and flexible manner in order that certain theatrical necessities, become an option for the cinema, should nevertheless not restrict the latter's freedom but rather enhance it.

1. Rarefaction of the settings. The principal setting in *Ordet*, Borgensgaard, is both enclosed in its unity (by the shots showing it from outside) and articulated as separate cells—different rooms—whose constellation is oriented, in the very image of a family hearth, by a central communal room. A setting ceaselessly explored, exploited in whole or in part—Who will finally put the myth of Dreyer's immobile camera out of its misery? ("It is important to have a live and mobile camera fluidly following the characters, even on a close-up, so that the décor constantly changes place": Dreyer, *Cahiers*, nr. 127).

2. Density of the characters. Here concerned less with any solemnity or hieratic manner as a priori formal system of emphases (being "theatrical") than, in the case of the Borgen grandfather and his daughter-in-law Inger, with the tangibly rendered reality (Inger's marvellous movements as she bakes) of the peasant-aristocracy nature of the characters. As for the authority of Johannes the fool, it comes paradoxically from a sort of absence of weight in him—as though his own absentness made his authority more weighty—from the eventuality of a levitation.

3. Speech as substance of the film. A speech in the literal, edifying sense which, from word to word makes both spectator and film hang on its enunciation.

The most remarkable thing about *Ordet*, however, is that the spoken word (of which it has been perhaps too often said, making facile reference to the mystical connotations of The Word, that it is the subject of the film) is not in fact equally weighted and saturated with meaning throughout the film. Doubtless the tone at times became overweighted, momentous, and lest it become too much so and therefore meaningless, had to be interrupted by an astonishing number of scenes in which the characters drink coffee, or have its solemnity counteracted by the homespun simplicity of a kitchen, the crudity of a pigsty. To this end, Dreyer (as he has himself explained: see *Cahiers*, nrs. 127 and 170) also employs a technique of decompressing speech—here, by simplifying the dialogue from the play—which acknowledges the different kind of word space in the cinema: the shot space, which limits more or less to its duration the different verbal remanences—sound, emotion, music. Hence the simplicity of the Word in *Ordet*.

4. Abstraction. The theatre is more abstract than the cinema: a commonplace whose ineptitude Dreyer demonstrates by making his film even more abstract than Kaj Munk's play, which he reduces to a scenario highly theoretical in structure, restricted to two dimensions:

—One is vertical: the contrast between the tailor's dark Christianity and the grandfather's enlightened faith, with between them a sort of tertiary religious sector where two apathies meet: the functional ministry of the pastor, and the hesitant rationalism of the doctor.

—The other is horizontal, within the Borgensgaard farm, where the grandfather's faith is countered by the three forms of religious aberration—misalliance, atheism, mystical mania—perpetrated by his three sons. "The talking picture is thus seen to be like a play in concentrated form" (Dreyer, *Cahiers* nr. 127).'

The diegesis of this film is open to a number of contradictory readings. For instance Bjorn Rasmussen, in the magazine *Catholica* (1955), asserts that the film will serve Christianity more because 'Dreyer has depicted the miracle of faith without giving in to the sneaking underlying doubt one always finds a trace of in the poet [Kaj Munk] himself'. For Rasmussen the necessary faith which both 'bright' and 'dark' interpretations of Christianity lack is provided for in the final scene by the child's faith in her uncle Johannes. The film, he says, is a 'simply sublime' sermon.

Rather, what seems to me very clear in this film is the persistence of a certain aspect

66

of the fantastic which I described in relation to *Vampyr*, *i.e.* the uncertainty—principle. Are the events miraculous, do they represent divine intervention, or is there a 'rational' explanation? The text is very carefully constructed around a range of positions: from the scientific rationalism of the doctor to Inger and her child's belief in daily miracles, via Mikkel Borgen's stubborn unbelief and the preacher's scepticism. In a sense, it is the doctor who is most prepared to accept the 'resurrection' because of its challenge to the explanatory schemes of modern science. Dreyer also makes this point somewhere in an interview when he claims that new perspectives have been opened up by the relativity theory 'that make us realise a deep connection between exact science and intuitive religion. The new science brings us closer to a deeper understanding of the divine and is well on the way to giving a natural explanation for supernatural things.' This uncertainty is foregrounded, for instance, when the doctor's car leaves, the light from his headlamps throwing a shadow on the door leading to Inger's room. Is this merely a shadow or is it, as Johannes thinks, the scythe of Death.

*　　*　　*

1961 Gertrud

Production	Palladium Film
Script	Dreyer. Based on the play by Hjalmar Söderberg.
Director of Photography	Henning Bendtsen
Art Director	Kaj Rasch
Music	Jørgen Jersild
Songs	Grethe Risbjerg Thomsen
Editor	Edith Schlüssel

Nina Pens Rode (*Gertrud*), Bendt Rothe (*Gustav Kanning*), Ebbe Rode (*Gabriel Lidman*), Baard Owe (*Erland Jansson*), Axel Strøbye (*Axel Nygren*), Vera Gebuhr (*The Kannings' maid*), Anna Malberg (*Kanning's mother*), Eduard Mielche (*The Rector Magnificus*).
Running time: 115 mins.

Regarding his choice of subject matter, Dreyer said in an interview published in *Films and Filming* (Vol.7, nr. 9):

'I had chosen the work of Hjalmar Söderberg because his conception of tragedy is more modern, he was overshadowed far too long by the other giants, Ibsen and Strindberg. Why did I say he was "more modern"? Well, instead of suicide and other grand gestures in the tradition of pathetic tragedy, Söderberg preferred the bitter tragedy of having to go on living even though ideals and happiness have been destroyed . . . But what is so fascinating about Söderberg, and I think you can apply it to our present-day society, is that conflicts materialise out of apparently trivial conversations. In simple terms, his characters frequently fail to communicate, and mean different things with the *same* words. The doctrines of love held by Gertrud might be interpreted to mean "Love is all . . . Either her ideal of love fully realised or else loneliness" . . . I think we shall see the new generation giving greater recognition to the genius of Söderberg.'

Dreyer absolutely rejects any accusations of 'artificiality' in relation to *Gertrud*:
'Obviously, the dialogue is not artificial! I simply wanted to make a film that is

set in a certain period—the turn of the century—and that unfolds in a well-defined milieu. It is therefore certain that the language reflects something of this time and this milieu, that it possesses a special coloration. Good actors understand the necessity for this work. They know that poetic phrases must be brought out in a certain fashion, with a certain rhythm, and every day speech in another fashion. And it is not only the tone that is concerned.

If you are in front of a screen, at the cinema, you have the tendency to follow everything that unfolds on it, which is different from the theatre where the words move through space and exist there, hanging in the air. At the cinema, as soon as they left the screen, the words die. Therefore I tried to make little pauses in order to give the spectator the possibility of assimilating what he hears, of thinking about it. That gives the dialogue a certain rhythm, a certain style.

In addition, it is a proof of stupidity not to recognise the very important role of the dialogue. Each subject implies a certain voice. And one must pay attention to that. And it is necessary to find a possibility for expressing the voice as much as one can. It is very dangerous to limit oneself to a certain form, a certain style.

I would very much like to have made *Gertrud* in colour. I even had a certain Swedish painter in mind, who has studied the period in which the film takes place and who has made many drawings and paintings in which he utilises very special colours.

The painter of whom I speak, whose name is Halman, above all does drawings for newspapers. You know, these big coloured pages for the Sunday edition. It is very pretty and done with very few colours. Four or five at the most. It is in that spirit that I would have wanted to do *Gertrud*. Soft colours, few in number, that go well together.

The main essay in this booklet devotes quite a lot of attention to *Gertrud*, and to avoid repeating myself, I would like to quote, *in extenso*, André Techiné's perceptive review of the film:

'After a long silence, Dreyer begins to speak. No need to wonder whether this is a testament or a summing-up: the simple fact that he has taken the floor suffices to warrant our attention. We know from Blanchot that speech replaces the concrete by an essential equilibrium close to immobility. Structured in separate fragments, the film imposes an initial perspective. Indeed, this structure decants the dramatic effect in that it proclaims through highly allusive verses what colouring the events presented will assume. The apparent chronology of the narrative introduces no inflections to its unfolding. There is really no evolution or succession, because the present is never lived as it emerges but as it is spoken, *i.e.* already thought. Man leaves his passions to turn to words. The gesture accomplished by the actors clearly indicates this intention. Being preeminently a peaceful gesture, the act of sitting down permits a recuperation of forces, a certain detachment that impels the voices to take stock. In the way the decor is used, the seat becomes the stimulant element: the benches in the park, the rim of a fountain, the various armchairs, even the stool at the end. The film space in which the characters talk is never in direct contact with Nature, with the apparent exception of the scene in the park, but "The nature found in gardens is not the country meadow but an evocation, an artifice, a dream; it should be added that the dream develops only on condition that the person strolling through it moves as though conducted by music". (Baltrusaitis and Starobinski.)

Everything happens in interiors, indeed in "chamber" (as one would say of music), because these figures considered in their totality plastically incarnate all possible landscapes. "You are the moon, the sky, the sea..."** According to the process to which Dreyer has remained faithful, filming an attitude, a facial tremor, is enough to open perspectives instead of closing them. It is not so much the amplification as the reduction which liberates and suspends the meaning. Corresponding to the constant hierographic impulse traversing the bodies is the call to song as the culmination of speech. Directed towards a seat, a movement abolishes the nature of the decor as "appliance", purifies it of any functional element. And the speech instigated is no longer purposive, is no longer addressed to the real considered as a field of action, but sets up a sort of echo, a sound capsule of troubles lived and therefore past. The words are no longer pronounced but effaced by the preponderance of rhythmic fluidity. Perhaps this vocalisation should be compared to the modulation effected by Mizoguchi in *The Empress Yang Kwei Fei* (but not in *Sansho the Bailiff* or *Ugetsu Monogatari*, because the kingdom of man is no longer the only one apprehended).

The film makes visible the final stages of the acquisition of the order of language, acknowledging the living movement from which it has become detached and with which it will never again merge. This is not so much dream as the death of another life, slowed down, equable, continuing, as though cast off. Until the body, itself speaking, finally disappears in the final absence of decor, or lingers as a landmark, a springboard, a trace.

As for Dreyer's modernity, perhaps the open doors should be battered down since they are not open to all. Like Mankiewicz, Guitry or Godard (for example), unlike Cacoyannis (*Electra*) or Yutkevitch (*Othello*) among others, Dreyer proves that the physical approach to speech is the business of cinema and therefore of man, and that an attentive eye on two figures talking even in a prolonged and static shot will never cease to astonish us.'

*   *   *

C. Work as scriptwriter
1912
Bryggerens Datter (Dir.: Rasmus Ottesen)

1913
Balloneksplosionen (Dir.: unknown)
Krigskorrespondenten (Dir.: unknown)
Hans og Grethe (Dir.: Wolder)
Chatollets Hemmelighed (Dir.: Hjalmar Davidsen)

1914
Ned med Vaabnene (Dir.: Holger-Madsen)
Penge (Dir.: Karl Mantzius)
Pavillonens Hemmelighed (Dir.: Karl Mantzius)

Editorial Notes
*Society For Education in Film and Television.
**See the second editorial note of *Appendix I*.

1915
Juvelerernes Skraek (Dir.: A. Christian)
Den Hvide Djævel (Dir.: Holger-Madsen)
Den Skønne Evelyn (Dir.: A. W. Sandburg)
Rovedderkoppen (Dir.: August Blom)
En Forbryders Liv og Levned (Dir.: A. Christian)
Guldets Gift (Dir.: Holger-Madsen)

1916
Den Mystiske Selskabsdame (Dir.: August Blom)
Hans Rigtige Kone (Dir.: Holger-Madsen)
Fange No. 113 (Dir.: Holger-Madsen)
Lydia (Dir.: Holger-Madsen)
Glædens Dag (Dir.: A. Christian)
Gillekop (Dir.: August Blom)

1917
Hotel Paradis (Dir.: Robert Dinesen)

1918
Grevindens Ære (Dir.: August Blom)

1947
De Gamle (Dir.: T. A. Svendsen)

1950
Shakespeare Og Kronborg (Dir.: Jørgen Roos)

1954
Rønnes og Nexøs Genopbygning (Dir.: Poul Bang)

1956
Noget om Norden (Dir.: Bent Barfod)

*   *   *

D. Other work

Dreyer worked as editor on a short film, directed by Otto Schray, entitled *Radioens Barndom, The Childhood of Radio* (1949), and later, 1956, Bent Barfod wrote and directed a short film based on an idea by Dreyer: *Noget om Norden (Something Happening in the North)*.

Among his unrealised projects, perhaps the most important one was a film to be called *Jesus fra Nasaret.*

Dreyer spent a considerable amount of time and energy after the war trying to set up a film on the life of Christ. Many producers were interested, including J. Arthur Rank, and it is not clear why the film was not made, since the money appears to have been available.

Dreyer went to Israel to study the locale, and taught himself Hebrew. In the

70

scenario, Palestine is a country occupied by foreign aggressors, as Denmark was under the Nazi's when he first conceived of the project. The Zealots are presented as resistance fighters, the Pharisees as supporters of the *status quo*, and the upper-class Saducees as collaborators with the Romans.

Jesus is portrayed as a politically inactive, mild mannered Rabbi, forced into leadership by the oppressed. Since witnessing the persecution of European Jews by the Nazi's, Dreyer became concerned to show that the Romans rather than the Jews were responsible for the crucifixion.

Other projects included an adaptation of Euripides' *Medea*, Faulkner's *Light in August*, O'Neill's *Mourning becomes Electra*, Ibsen's *Brand*, Strindberg's *Damascus*, and a film on *Mary, Queen of Scots*.

Appendix 1

The Nordic Archaism of Dreyer
by André Techiné

> 'A man walking along was casting his shadow, and one could not tell
> which was the man and which the shadow, nor how much shadow he
> cast.'
>
> (Yeats)*

It isn't always easy to recognise in passing certain premonitory signs
catering to the urgent interrogation the cinema as a whole is subjected to by
each film. It can even happen that this purely interrogative relationship
maintained by each individual film with the seventh art in general is not only
modified but defined in other terms. Nothing is more fugitive and suspect
than an innovatory conception of no matter what means of expression. For
the theory of novelty rests directly on a need not to be left defenceless, when
in fact everything ineluctably passes us by. Our inability to encompass what
has been contributed is demonstrated along with clear evidence of these
contributions. An elucidation then attempted can only be a wrong approach,
falsified from the outset by the need to refer, even for the purpose of
rejecting it, to a scale of values that is already outdated. Film-makers are like
guests. Some appear at the appointed time, as expected, fulfilling or
disappointing our hopes.

Others arrive at the last moment, unannounced, dismaying the assembled
company by presenting them with an unfamiliar or simply forgotten face.
Then whatever means one has to hand are used to place the newcomer. Eyes
firmly fixed on the quest for modernity at all costs, we have seen the
unexpected suddenly turn up—unexpected enough, at any rate, for us to be
unable to foresee that it would succeed in disrupting our closed circuit
debate. A man from the north has come to talk to us and to talk of cinema, not
the cinema as we know it but the cinema as he knows it. Not of documentary
(that is, elimination of the expressive through the ambivalence of the
expression), not of construction (that is, participation in the expressive
through the effectiveness of the expression), but of rudiments. For there is
no film-maker more rudimentary than Dreyer. Unqualified to lay down the
law or to pressurise in any way, Dreyer makes talking pictures considered
and reconsidered strictly subject to the means he employs or, if you prefer,
the elements on which they are founded.

Each new film is not approached as an isolated venture having only distant resemblances to past experiences, but as a voyage of discovery constantly penetrating deeper, an investigation that constantly becomes more exacting. Dreyer exhausts the resources of his own vocabulary, working his material until all resistance is overcome and he contrives to mould the scant and stubborn forces with which he set out and to which he limits himself. For what Dreyer accepts, or to be more precise acquires, is a refusal to resort to the appurtenances, details, incidental hurdles, external flourishes and irrelevant variations, the whole gamut of effects offered by an expedient rhetoric.

So manifest an absence of elegance and virtuosity may lead one to think that Dreyer's range is seriously lacking in scope. But this poverty purely and simply indicates the only riches possible in Dreyer's view: those of discovery and of creation. Instead of taking up and integrating the successive modifications sustained by an aggregate of signs considered in an evolutive perspective, Dreyer sets up his own independent system and steadfastly sticks to it, permitting no borrowings. If he is commonly assumed to be outdated as a film-maker, it is because each of his films demonstrates his insistence on marking out a distinctive cinematic policy that remains resolutely aloof from other concurrent discoveries. This does not mean that influences are non-existent (that of Griffith is even acknowledged). Nor does it mean that Dreyer has established a language all on his own. He remains dependent upon the cinema, but does not acknowledge its evolution or take it into consideration except where the change is radical (for instance, the passage from silents to sound). In that case, faced by a different means of expression, he adopts and moulds it to his own use. 'A reorganisation and a simplification are necessary. One can, if you like, say that it's a question of purification because all elements not engaged in the central idea are suppressed. One concentrates and one compresses.' This strict reduction is effected with the object of commanding increasingly precisely a specific articulation. It sets up a sort of univocal, indeed autonomous, field of action. A divestment as ruthless as this infallibly throws into relief its configuration, lays it bare in other words, reveals its mechanism. There is a scheme, a sort of architecture exhibiting, contrary to an apparent complexity (as is the case with Lang, for instance), an extreme simplification. This simplification enables one to pick out the elements Dreyer has at his disposal and which he contents himself with developing. It is hardly the result of an omission—from any lack of consideration, that is— but on the contrary of a structuring in the most artisanal sense of the term; of an accretion, in other words, a selective montage. Dreyer learns his art by experience, staking out his path to restrict it more surely and reinforce it even more strongly than before. For the elementary sketch the creator arrives at without application or verification of fundamental rules is attained only by way of tentative efforts and approaches. But wouldn't the nordic archaism show itself somewhere in this broadly outlined, simply made sketch? Wouldn't the schema reveal an ambiguity deeper than the

73

implications carried by all the innovations descending from too freshly acquired cultural heritages?

Faces and setting, by preference enclosed, are immediately apparent as firmly delineated guidelines, not contenting themselves with organising the sketch according to an established geometry but setting up—at the risk of some imperceptible disturbance—an irreducible dynamic. This impulse, skilfully regulated from within by an arrangement in which each element predisposes in favour of immobility, introduces the narrative force that is at once tranquil and menacing. For at the heart of a system as rigorous as this, at the centre of so meticulous a structure, the least vibration figures as an uncertain gravitation, and an equilibrium disturbed and causing a divergence in the contours. The blink of an eyelid, a gesture by a hand, become irretrievable. Because they incessantly elude the schematism that provokes and haunts them at every moment. Because they vaguely trace an élan one thought not possible here, and which is seen to persist, an outcropping on the surface of volumes. Joan's naked face is presented to the spectator quite independently of any psychological or dramatic determination. By dint of grimaces and contorted expressions, the precise intentions (fear, joy, grief) disappear or melt away, obscuring the message so as to leave only a transparent face which at each blink of the eyes yields indeterminate indications that no precise significance can cover. A denotational impossibility as acute as this shows the extent to which so rudimentary an art can lead to ambiguity, instantly establishing a free relationship with the spectator. For the means employed (and their economy should again be stressed) are entrusted not with a decorative role but, on the contrary, a 'generative' one. Speech and expressions do not reduce the perspectives, do not make the dimensions narrower, but open horizons, engender possibilities. The elements (easily enumerated) comprise a diffuse, latent plurality of 'imaging functions'. The sign, in its entirely primitive crudity and clarity, never in fact ceases to foster allusions. During the progress of an action systematically condensed in time and decanted by a schematic disposition into tableaux, the ponderous speech effaces itself between four walls and a woman's face even in the cinema as it is today, just as the extravagant communications on Joan's face effaced themselves in the silent days. For Dreyer proposes precise forms only in so far as they conjure imprecisions. When he films a figure sitting in an armchair, one sees 'the moon, the sea, the forest', as one of the characters says while looking at Gertrud.** Reverie is sparked off by a gesture or a look, as though conducted by music and propagating itself against an inner background stripped to the point of abstraction. 'My only desire is to show the world of the imagination,' Dreyer says. In this respect *Vampyr* accumulated in the course of its progress every imaginable opening independently of any coherence. The level, however, may seem somewhat incidental in this sombrely surreal story. This melodic oneirism requires a rigid framework before it can come into being and venture its modulations. *Two People*, on the other hand, stifles the rhythmic fluidity beneath a framework whose density encroaches too much. But in either extreme the equilibrium has nothing to do with careful proportionment, compromises, precautions. Dreyer is not a stylist. He uses the cinema, or rather invents his cinema in order to imagine life through feminine characters bruised in their passions and disappointed in their dreams (Anne in *Day of Wrath*, Inger in *Ordet*, Marianne in *Two People*, and Gertrud). For dreams are more important to nordic than mediterranean peoples. The hearth convenes, whereas the sun disperses. When night comes, the old man tells his stories and finds the right words. There is no literature. In the warm interior one can talk slowly of the seasons, of new beginnings. What we learn from Dreyer is that one must be attentive to the apportionment of light, to the landscape fleetingly glimpsed in Gertrud's eyes, to the world that rocks as a voice dies away.

Rudimentary, solitary, timeless, Dreyer owes nothing to anyone and seems to owe nothing to the cinema itself. If one wants to see what is going on in the seventh art one must look elsewhere. Whereas Rossellini or American films are informative about certain conditions in cinema, here there is no guide.

In the cold north it seems that long evenings spent in company are pleasant and never-ending. This is how Dreyer's stories come down to us. And instead of talking, or indeed through talking, the voice of the storyteller lingers on saying it is listening to us.

From *Cahiers du cinéma*, nr. 170. Transl.: Tom Milne

Editorial notes:
*The quote from Yeats has been re-translated from French.
**Techiné slightly mis-remembers the scene in question. It is Gertrud herself who speaks. For a more accurate rendering of the words spoken, see p. 26.

Appendix 2

Spiritual Men and Natural Women.[1]
By Frieda Grafe

There should be so many pictures on this page that written words could only advance in fits and starts. Stills which break through the text, just as in Dreyer's films holes are broken in the walls by objects hung upon them, by mirrors, pictures and windows. Pictures of tribunals, secular and ecclesiastical, of councils of men sitting in judgement on child-murderers, witches and saints; of fathers giving away their daughters in marriage according to their own ideals. Also pictures of texts which, obstinately and violently, arrest the flow of film images again and again: decrees, judgements, instructions on how to deal with a vampire by driving a stake through its heart at midnight. And poems, the love poems in *Gertrud* singing of things which can only exist in the realms of poetic freedom.

Then, often, there are pictures of men's outstreched arms holding wool so that women can wind it up into balls more easily. Another picture: a bride and bridegroom eating from one pot: with two spoons chained together. And the table with the check oil cloth in *Ordet* where Inger rolls out her pastry and on which she later lies giving birth to her still-born son. And finally the last shot from Dreyer's last film: a white door in a white wall which Gertrud, white haired and already half a ghost, has just shut behind her. She can no longer bear to hear the sterile men's talk of duty, honour, labour, law and passion. The highest concepts, and in Nietzsche's view the most general and the emptiest, 'the last puff of smoke of the most attenuated reality'.

Gertrud had taken the concepts at their face value and wanted to fill them with life. She was an inconvenience. She could not understand that Law and Reality are opponents, that by their very natures they belong to different worlds.

A Sieve-like Space

Dreyer said that he was particularly attracted by white walls, and there are white walls in nearly all of his films. One can see white walls coming into being in *Vampyr* where the rhythmic flow of the floor becomes a prison, a trap and a grave for the old doctor. For Dreyer, white walls consist of a multitude of glowing, transparent, tiny fragments. Reality becomes diaphanous: contours and stable features dissolve. The material develops a life of its own—in *Vampyr* the quality of the light and the structure resulting from it is due to a mistake in the copying laboratory. *Vampyr* should be seen after *Michael*, a film version of the Hermann Bang novel, which tells the story of a painter-prince who lives his life as if on the stage. With him the 19th century and with it Idealism have shut their last window and lie down to die.

In *Michael* there is a view of nature and of landscape, functioning as an undercurrent, threatening all around it. *Vampyr* gives shape to the consequences of this: the pictures of the end of the 19th century are dissolved and superceeded by the images of the cinema.

It is unimportant to establish whether Dreyer was conscious of a change of epochs. His films bear its imprint. They are corridors, transitional worlds. One is so clearly aware of what moves his figures because he lets the actors move slowly, and the camera as well. One has time to hear the words, to explore the spaces. Dreyer said that he let speeches occur in close-ups, (and that he filmed theatre,) so that cinema could bring theatre through and beyond itself.

Before they are exchange of meanings, his dialogues are modulations, musically overdetermined, a multitude of accents. That part of speech which is expressed in echo: its end—in *Vampyr*, or in *Ordet* where the mad Johannes quotes the Bible in a voice like cotton-wool and expressionlessly repeats words and sentences. And in *Gertrud* there are the moans of the men. Its beginning is in *Day of Wrath*; the raw state is the child-like scream of the old woman, penetrating from the attic into the presbytery below, when the constables capture her to bring her to trial as a witch.

Between them lies the intrinsic realm of language, order, spoken order. Where all that is permitted is what appears to be clear, unambiguous and can be checked, the world of judicial enquiry, of the *procès-verbal*, where it is always the same sentences which must be proffered if justice is to be maintained and order upheld. Of *Joan of Arc* with its succession of close-ups, the purest and most cinematographic of all his films, Dreyer has said that it is a film about language, about language as a means of torture, about the terrorism of language.

Too much honour

In Dreyer's films the representatives of the Word form a strange sect. The bearers of the Word are holders of spiritual office: priests, judges, family tyrants, homosexual foster fathers, and artists with words, poets. The Danish title for *Master of the House* is, literally, *Thou Shalt Honour Thy Wife*. The story of the head of a family, broken by the three women who formed him: his mother, his old nurse and his wife. Dreyer brings forms onto the screen that have no other function than to make understandable the structures lying beneath them and generating them. As one watches the film one does not notice that there is still a little sympathy remaining for this rather repulsive patriarch. But his mournful face gives us a clue. Whereas all the rest of the family are constantly conspiring with one another, he is always the great outsider. His exclusion is not the result of his detestable behaviour, it is just that his position as a father places excessive demands upon him.

The film is about the often cited role playing of men who become fathers against their wills, because they are born into Symbolic systems which they are unable to assume and embody. For Dreyer the father, the defender of Order, is overwhelmed by his own prestige, by what his place, his social position in the widest sense, demands of him: the father in *The President* and the father in *Day of Wrath* who have to be both father to their family and to their community. When the two fathers in *Ordet* quarrel over the children whose marriage the older generation want to prevent because of religious differences, two mongrels can be heard fighting in the background.

They justify their behaviour In The Name of the Father, not in terms of the paternity which is in fact their's. The Symbolic Order places its stamp upon the real. Gertrud opposes them both by refusing to have any name, either that of her father, or that of her husband, cut upon her gravestone. All she allows is *Amor Omnia*. She wanted, finally, to be herself and only herself. The mirror that men had given her and that they had loved was a prop she found she no longer needed.

Gertrud is the invention of a man; rather the invention of two men since the film was based on a play by Hjalmar Söderberg. Like many of Dreyer's women, Gertrud is a statue, a memorial. Her demands are as absolute as the contours of the film, its spaces and the gestures of the figures in it are hard and angular. Her demands are too idealistic, a sign of their detour through men. But sometimes one can hear the russle of the long dresses: some little intimacy is established. And then she travels off to Paris to study with Charcot, Freud's teacher. The real name in the fictitious context operates as a breakthrough, which can be compared with the pictures of nature in *Michael*. An order, long valid, is challenged. Reality announces the appearance of a new dimension.

The return of the repressed

What then appears was not dead, merely covered over; invisible because of the sediments of deliberate and cautious conventions. Age-old but still changing, that is *The Parson's Widow*. The elderly pastor's wife, getting into her fourth marriage with a good-for-nothing (who has a mistress of his own) because the job is tied to her person, shakes off everything that life had provided her with just as that life is drawing to a close. From being an object of exchange, an object amid other objects upon which she is dependent, because, as she puts it, they are her life, she finds the way back to the feelings of her youth. To the astonishment of those around her, she leaves the house more and more often to visit the grave of her first husband who she links with feelings which she rediscovers in the two young swindlers.

The virulence of the subject is increased by the humour of the film, which is an important element in the undermining of any fixed positions one may feel inclined to adopt. The end of the film is, indeed, terrible, horrifying—

horrifying as only a Dreyer film can be. The old woman dies and the young one is seen trying on her clothes.

Even the most frightening of the mother figures, the self denying old Merete in *Day of Wrath*, more papal than the Pope himself when it comes to defending the laws of a man's world, has weaker moments when she is unable to maintain her poise. When she finds her son dead, a completely different aspect is revealed alongside that of the character of the figurehead of the parsonage. Something which reminds us of the mild old witch whose death at the stake she had deemed to be just.

In a paper written in 1926, Freud states that the sexual life of women is a *dark continent* for psychology, and it seems all the darker as this is the only English expression to be found in the entire text. By this he meant less what Wilhelm Reich was to stress later: the threat and danger to authoritarian ideology posed by women if their right to sexuality were to be officially recognised. What concerned Freud more was the fact that femininity evaded the possibility of representation: sublimation. The fact that female sexuality did not conform to the laws of repression, so that its restraint required stronger censorship.

Anne, the young witch in *Day of Wrath* is married to a much older man. The most perverse and poorest of priests, who, after the death of his first wife used the power of his position to get himself a young bride. From his first marriage he has a son, the same age as his young wife, who he has never touched. And when the son appears the system begins to crack: the succession of the generations begins to become confused. Anne is merely the weak link in the chain. Nature breaks through the covering layers of culture. 'In the Bible, as in all traditional systems of law, the confusion of the succession from one generation to another is accursed . . .' One feels how the danger slowly mounts: a harmless game of hide-and-seek at the beginning to surprise the old pastor is the start of deception, the original sin.

At her trial Anne admits to having witches' powers only when she sees her love betrayed by the man returning to conformity within the paternal order. Where there was a difference, a contradiction, harmony reigns once more. The burning of the young woman at the stake is eased by choirboys singing the *Dies Irae*.

Interior Exterior

The fissure which yawns for a moment, the disorder which spreads, the danger to the law, reveal the basis on which order rests. *Maître* (master) is to this day a french synonym for lawyer. In *Michael*, the painter-prince is addressed as master, and his mastery comes to an end because Nature casts it aside. Shut the window, the painter says to his servant, and as he does so, the last trace of the external world vanishes from his studio. In *Michael*, the entry of Nature is linked with the entry of Woman; She is natural, Baudelaire said, and that means abominable. Dreyer lets one recognise that the nature of Woman can accommodate all forms of masquerade. As Princess Zamikow in *Michael*, Nora Gregor is in fact a scarecrow.

To look behind things is not for Dreyer a matter of seeking their ideal depths. Their beyond is not, as with Fritz Lang, the underground, the paths, cavities and dungeons under the earth. It operates on the same level as the visible. The crucial thing is not what is behind the images, but what is visible in them as a speck of white. The beyond of Dreyer's films, which he often hides behind historical materials or period dress is the repressed, censored portion of the 'this-side' of things. 'I build houses', complains the mad Johannes in *Ordet*, 'in which no one wants to live', taking two lit candelabra and putting them in the window. Gertrud could say exactly the same thing.

Often it seems that Dreyer's mystical themes are in total conflict with the realistic nature of his medium. True, at times Dreyer acts like a wizard, like Anne in *Day of Wrath* when she tries out her supernatural powers and finds to her astonishment and terror that they work.

Dreyer uses cinema to wake the dead. But to follow him, one must go a step further. he uses cinema not just to show reality, but also the sign-laden nature of reality, he makes the Symbolic Order and its constriants visible. He changes the normal relation between sign and idéa. With his insistence upon objects and the imperviousness of the body, he protests against the notion of the total translatability of everything into everything else. For him there is something that the symbol, the cycle of representation, misses. 'Labour' wrote Marx, 'is not the only source of material abundance, it is its father, and the earth its mother'. When Inger dies in *Ordet*, the father tries to comfort his son with the idea that she is in heaven, but the son, uncomforted, replies: 'But it was her body that I loved as well'.

The centre of Dreyer's films never appears directly. Only its outline is marked. The images are only scraps of the infinite, of the unformed, the possible, hieratically and rigidly demonstrating their own limitations. One can never wholly identify with any single figure in a Dreyer film: there are no heroes and no villains. The conflicts are cosmic but not historical. Different types of order clash with one another, or rather order clashes with disorder. One should not be misled by the quietism of the endings of many of his films. They arouse anger. And when one thinks of the miracle at the end of *Ordet*, the raising of the dead, that is in fact the real triumph of disorder.

An event beyond all interpretability, outside any context. A zero point, another white speck, a gap in the chain of causality. When Freud began to describe the Unconscious and to comprehend it in a theoretical manner he could only establish that he was in an area where the conceptual apparatus of the existing sciences broke down. That it was the great Other on which we all depend, and which, at first, could only be conceptualised by means of negative categories.

When one sees Dreyer's films today one is often struck by the thought that they are not of this world. When, at Dreyer's request, *Gertrud* had its first showing in Paris in 1964, the audience was numb with horror. Pathetically, they tried to explain away what they had seen by saying that Dreyer had become totally senile. The film was utterly different from what had been expected, had nothing to do with what one remembered of earlier Dreyer films. 'The actors', said Dreyer, 'are completely natural. They speak and move in a completely natural rhythm'. Once you have seen them, they can never be forgotten.[2]

From *Süddenstruhe Bertung*, 9/10 Feb. 1974

Editorial Notes

1. The German title could also be translated as *Priests and Natural Women*. Moreover, the author uses 'Hevien' and 'Damen', terms belonging to a more elevated and weighty semantic sphere than the everyday men and women ('ladies and gentlemen').
2. From *Im Off—Filmartikel*, by F. Grafe and E. Patalas, Carl Hanser Verlag, Munich 1974. First published in the *Süddeutsche Zeitung*, 9/10 Feb. 1974. Transl. by R. Mann.

Further Reading

The most useful collection of Dreyer's writings on film is *Dreyer in Double Reflection*, ed. Skoller, New York 1973; Tom Milne's *The Cinema of Carl Dreyer*, London 1971, is still the most useful for extended plot summaries and perceptive commentary on individual films. Since it is still in print I have tried not to overlap with this book so that readers interested in Dreyer will find it a useful complement to the present work.

Of the writing on individual films from the perspective of avant-garde/independent filmmakers, see: Burch and Dana, 'Positions', *Afterimage 5*. For a critique of their positions see the articles by Stephen Heath and myself in *Screen*, vol 17 nr 3.

There is a lot of material in foreign languages, particularly French and Italian, motivated primarily by the different functions of religious ideology in those countries. Good examples can be found in the short reviews by André Bazin in *Le cinéma de la cruauté*, Paris 1975. For detailed phenomenological accounts of the films see the special issue of *Etudes Cinématographiques* nr 53/6 by P. Parrain.

Regarding the screenplays of *Joan of Arc*, *Vampyr*, *Day of Wrath* and *Ordet* in *Four Screenplays*, London 1970, the reader should be warned that these are screenplays and bear only a very indirect relation to the actual film-texts as they exist on celluloid.

Printed in England by Brown Knight & Truscott Ltd. London & Tonbridge